THE STUDY OF MEDIEVAL GREEK ROMANCE

OPUSCULA GRAECOLATINA
Edenda curavit Ivan Boserup
Vol. 33

The Study of Medieval Greek Romance:
A Reassessment of Recent Work

by

Panagiotis A. Agapitos
&
Ole L. Smith

MUSEUM TUSCULANUM PRESS
University of Copenhagen 1992

© 1992 by Museum Tusculanum Press & the authors
Computer typeset by Ole L. Smith
Printed in Denmark at Special-Trykkeriet Viborg a-s
ISBN 87 7289 163 7
ISSN 0107 8089

Supported by the Faculty of Humanities, University of Copenhagen

Front cover: Hero killing a fantastic beast.
Glazed pottery dish (12th-13th Century),
Hermitage Museum (Petersburg, *olim* Leningrad).

MUSEUM TUSCULANUM PRESS
University of Copenhagen
92-94 Njalsgade
DK-2300 Copenhagen S.

Contents

Foreword 7
Preface 9
Introduction 12
Chapter 1: The twelfth-century background 15
Chapter 2: The literary tradition 22
Chapter 3: The proto-romance, Digenis Akritis 26
Chapter 4: The renaissance of a genre 34
Chapter 6: The first »modern Greek« literature 45
Chapter 7: The original romances: the texts and the stories 50
Chapter 9: Translations and adaptations of Western romances 65
Chapter 10: Genealogy of the romances 73
Chapter 11: Common elements of the romances 91
Chapter 12: Reception 102
Epilogue 112
Bibliography 114
Index locorum 125
Subject index 127

ἀγαθὴ δ' ἔρις ἥδε βροτοῖσιν
Hesiod, *Op.* 24

Foreword

Over the past years a substantial number of publications on Byzantine vernacular literature have appeared. The scope of the various studies ranges from new critical editions to literary interpretations of different directions. This trend, to which both Byzantinists and Neohellenists are contributing, found a first peak in the organization of the Cologne conference 'Neograeca Medii Aevi' in 1986. The continuing interest is happily reflected in the organization of a 'Neograeca Medii Aevi ii' by the Greek Institute of Byzantine and post-Byzantine Studies in Venice this very year. Among the vernacular texts the Palaiologian romances have been favoured by scholars, while the appearance of the book-length study by Roderick Beaton, *The Medieval Greek Romance* [Cambridge Studies in Medieval Literature 6] (Cambridge 1989), where both the Komnenian and the Palaiologian texts are discussed at length, testifies for the preference.

The authors of the present study, who have their own share in this general interest concerning the vernacular romances, picked up Professor Beaton's book with eager expectation. In the course of our reading, however, we formed some substantial disagreements with the author. These disagreements became the moving force to examine in depth the presentation of the problems, the method involved, the general conclusions drawn by the author and juxtapose them with our own experience from studying these texts. That the results are to a high degree opposing and contradicting Beaton's presentation will surely be profitable for other students in the field. In this sense we pick up the author's own suggestion to other scholars: 'Where they find that I have disagreed with them in the ensuing pages I hope that they will respond in the spirit of open and continuing debate in which my own remarks are intended' (p. xii), a spirit which the Byzantines themselves found most agreeable when it came to intellectual matters.

The study follows in its structure the chapter organization of Beaton's book. Therefore, Chapter 1 does not mean our Chapter 1 but Beaton's. We have tried to present his views as complete as possible in order to make the reading of our text independent and internally coherent, hoping that it will not appear too esoteric to a reader who may not have been exposed to Beaton's book. However, two chapters have been omitted from our discussion, nos. 5 ('The twelfth-century texts') and 8 ('The original romances: narrative structure'). A critique of Beaton's interpretations of the Komnenian and Palaiologian texts would result in a large-scale interpretation of our own which is not the purpose of the present monograph. The interested reader may find some material in P. A. Agapitos, *Narrative Structure in the Byzantine Vernacular Romances. A Textual and Literary Study of* Kallimachos, Belthandros *and* Libistros [Miscellanea Byzantina Monacensia] (München 1991).

We would like to thank Daniel Ridings for invaluable support at the final critical stages of the production of the book.

Last but not least we wish to thank the Museum Tusculanum Press and in particular the editor of the series *Opuscula graecolatina,* Ivan Boserup, for their ready acceptance of our work. The Faculty of Arts in the University of Copenhagen came forward with a substantial grant without which our book could not have been published and we are deeply grateful for this support.

P. A. Agapitos, Athens
Ole L. Smith, Copenhagen and Gothenburg

Preface

In his *Preface*, after presenting in a categorical statement what the Byzantine romances are all about,[1] the author proceeds to expound the aims of his study and to sketch out the public to which this study is addressed. There are two main aims and two categories of readers. In the first category we find all those scholars who specialize in medieval literature, be it Western medievalists or Byzantinists. Here the author suggests that because of the lack of a 'systematic study of the Greek romances as a literary genre in any language... many of the questions addressed in this book may seem somewhat otiose to the Western medievalist used to relatively secure chronological and linguistic data, to consensus on editorial practice, and above all to the existence of modern scholarly editions' (xi). At the same time, he suggests that 'those working in the field of medieval Greek studies' could find such a study premature, on account of the absence of better editions and more analytical detail studies. 'In answer to the latter', the author continues, 'I believe that it will be difficult to progress much further in the vexed questions surrounding editorial method for many of these texts, until we can agree on the nature of the texts we are dealing with. One of the main aims of this book is therefore to propose a basis for such agreement'.

Unfortunately, both these points concerning Western medieval and Byzantine studies cannot be accepted. That there have been systematic studies (although one can argue over the definition of the term 'systematic') of Western vernacular literature cannot be doubted. That there is a consensus of opinion among Western medievalists on questions of editorial practice, dating, linguistic history etc. is not the case.[2] Moreover, there have been systematic presentations of the Byzantine romances, like Beck's analysis

---

[1] 'The Greek romances of the middle ages are tales of love, death and adventure' (xi). Plain numbers in parentheses refer to Beaton's book.

[2] For the disagreements on editorial practice see B. Cerquiglini, *Éloge de la variante. Histoire critique de la philologie* (Paris 1989) and *id.*, 'Variantes d'auteur et variance de copiste', in: L.Hay (ed.), *La naissance du texte* (Paris 1989) 105-119. For the highly contestable questions of secure linguistic data see Suzanne Fleischman, 'Philology, Linguistics and the Discourse of the Medieval Text', Speculum 65 (1990) 19-37. Concerning chronological difficulties see the discussion in *Fabliaux. Französische Schwankerzählungen des Hochmittelalters*. Ausgewählt, übersetzt und kommentiert von A. Gier (Stuttgart 1985) 309-313. One could also refer to the succinct account in Alfredo Stussi (ed.), *La critica del testo* (Bologna 1985) 7-31 which is a useful *aperçu* of the discussion in Romance philology.

in his *Volksliteratur,* Aleksidze's *Mir grečeskogo rycarskogo romana* or Hunger's *Hochsprachliche Literatur.*³ As for agreeing on the nature of the texts, how is it possible to understand this nature before the manuscripts preserving these texts have been dealt with in depth? For although, as the author himself acknowledges, there exists a fair amount of special studies concerning the works, their textual history and the codicological details of the manuscripts are far from elucidated. The available editions are almost in their entirety unsatisfactory and misleading.⁴ At the same time, and this in marked contrast to Western Medieval studies, broader analyses on aesthetic, cultural and hermeneutic questions of Byzantine literature are practically non-existant.⁵

Leaving the specialist behind, the author presents us with the second category of readers to whom the book is addressed, namely 'the non-specialist, and particularly scholars and students working comparatively on medieval literature' (xi-xii). Consequently, the book assumes the form of a comprehensive handbook which will present an overall view of these texts for non-specialists to use. This is not only a very highly set aim, but also a most difficult and responsible task, since a handbook must present in a clear and succinct form certified facts and not speculations. We shall examine at the end of

---

³ For details of these standards works see the Bibliography.

⁴ Perhaps it is proper to emphasize already here that existing editions of vernacular texts in general are unsatisfactory for a number of reasons. There is almost not one major text available in a modern reliable edition. M. K. Chatzigiakoumis, *Τὰ μεσαιωνικὰ δημώδη κείμενα. Συμβολὴ στὴ μελέτη καὶ τὴν ἔκδοσή τους. Α΄* : *Λίβιστρος, Καλλίμαχος, Βέλθανδρος* (Athens 1977) has now attempted to make scholars aware of this fact but he has so far only dealt with three of the texts and spelt out in detail the shortcomings of our 'standard' editions (Kriaras, Pichard, Lambert). Critics have pointed out defaults in some recent editions of vernacular texts, but even in the case of the highly questionable *Poulologos* text by Isabella Tsavari (*Ὁ Πουλολόγος. Κριτικὴ ἔκδοση μὲ εἰσαγωγή, σχόλια καὶ λεξιλόγιο* [Βυζαντινὴ καὶ νεοελληνικὴ βιβλιοθήκη 5] (Athens1987)) on which Hans Eideneier wrote a harsh though not unjustified critique (Südost-forschungen 47 [1988] 481-483), one must admit that it is now at least possible to see for oneself what the manuscripts have. It is only a few months ago that Eideneier published a new edition of the Ptochoprodromic poems, which gives at least one major vernacular text in a solid critical edition (see Hans Eideneier [Hrsg.], *Ptochoprodromos. Einführung, kritische Ausgabe, deutsche Übersetzung, Glossar* [Neograeca Medii Aevi 5] [Köln 1991]).

⁵ While for Western Medieval literature we have by now classical works like Erich Auerbach's *Mimesis* (1st edition Bern 1946) and E.R.Curtius' *Europäische Literatur und lateinisches Mittelalter* (1st edition Bern 1948), no such comparable studies are available to Byzantinists. For some restrained evaluations see H.-G. Beck, *Das literarische Schaffen der Byzantiner. Wege zu seinem Verständnis* [Sitzungsberichte der Österreichischen Akademie der Wissenschaften, philologisch-historische Klasse 229. 4] (Wien 1974); *id.*, *Das byzantinische Jahrtausend* (München 1978) 109-162; H. Hunger, 'On the Imitation (Μίμησις) of Antiquity in Byzantine Literature', Dumbarton Oaks Papers 23-24 (1969-1970) 17-38; *id.*, 'Die byzantinische Literatur der Komnenenzeit. Versuch einer Neubewertung', Anzeiger der philologisch-historischen Klasse der Österreichischen Akademie der Wissenschaften 105 (1968) 59-76. For a negative approach to Byzantine literature see C. Mango, *Byzantine Literature as a Distorting Mirror* (Oxford 1975).

our study whether the author has succeeded or not in his task.

Right at the beginning we are faced with a trivial but methodologically rather significant question, Beaton's introductory note on transliteration and citation in Greek (xiv-xv). For one thing: the most important task for a scholar is to highlight the diversity, the contradictory nature, the unevenness of his given subject. The attempt to gloss over the polymorphy of the raw material leads necessarily to simplification, generalization and the drawing of easy conclusions. The author chooses to transliterate learned and vernacular Byzantine texts as if they were Modern Greek. He also prints all the texts in the Modern Greek monotonic system, although this results in numerous inconsistencies and obscurities in the syntax of archaizing texts.[6]

---

[6] Especially when coupled with printers' errors in the Greek text, of which this book has its ample share. Cf. e.g. 64 αγάλματοί σε *Dros.* ii 248 (*recte* ἀγαλματοῖ σε).

Introduction

In the *Introduction* the reader is faced immediately with a proposition for 'unity': 16 works (including the *Erotokritos*) are presented as 'romances' in order 'to emphasize the links between most of them and similar literature in the west' (1). In this way the author preempts his concept, which is superimposed on a group of works with distinct individual features, displaying varied structural patterns and different linguistic registers. What Beaton began on the level of the printed text (unified system of transliteration and quotation of the original by modernizing it) is continued on the structural level of his study (unified point of view and system of reference).

The substitution of the term 'Byzantine', which purportedly emphasizes the differences with the west, creates a similar effect of false unity. Medieval Europe suddenly becomes a reflection of Modern Europe, a concept profoundly anachronistic and unsubstantiated by the sources both eastern and western. The author explains his 'unitarian' point of view by 'the new awareness in the twelfth century of a language community united by spoken Greek as well as by the literary inheritance from antiquity [which] is closely analogous to the developments underlying the rise of the vernacular literatures in the west' (1). This 'new awareness' - presented here as a factual statement - is developed in Chapter 1 and we will discuss it there in more detail. What should be said here, is that it is methodologically most dangerous to equate superficially similar historical processes, like 'the rise of the vernacular in east and west'. Furthermore, the notion of historical 'breaks' - like the often mentioned battle of Manzikert in 1071 (on which cf. below p. 15) - is to be taken with a grain of salt: the presupposition of historical awareness in periods where the mechanisms of historical analysis function completely differently and definitely not in socio-psychological terms (as defined in the 19th century and onwards) is not possible. Historical 'breaks' are of structural value for the modern scholar, but not for the medieval man. The Byzantines, for example, viewed time in universal terms by referring to a reconstructed date for the creation of the world but without any sense of the abstract quality of time calculation since they did their basic counting by the years of the undetermined indiction cycles.⁷

Beaton is then contradicting himself when he asks that 'the limit of 1453 is to be interpreted rather loosely' (2) for here the 'break' is not strongly marked. These allowances in the author's method reflect not so much his conceptual frame, as the actual lack of chronological evidence for most of these texts. Moreover, the notion of shifting cultural dominance within the 'evolution' of Medieval Greek romance-writing which Beaton implies (first Constantinople, then feudal Greece, then Venetian-ruled Crete) is unhistorical, since it presupposes exact developments within the already established 'unity' of the 16 'romances', a unity which cannot be so readily accepted.

The remainder of the *Introduction* presents a short sketch of the study of the romances in the last two centuries. However, the author does not really connect his choices of scholarly studies under discussion to the political and cultural developments of the 19th century. It is not enough to criticize previous scholars for their biased opinions. It is more important to understand the concepts underlying their particular points of view, because one gains in this way both a better insight in their work and in the object of study itself. For example, Beaton criticizes the fact that the Komnenian works are not mentioned in histories of Modern Greek literature (is on the other hand *Waltharius* quoted in histories of German literature?) or that the romances are assigned to different volumes in the *Byzantinisches Handbuch,* a point of view which completely misunderstands the structural concept of the various *Handbuch* volumes, superimposing again his sense of unity on the whole body of texts under consideration.⁸

The *Introduction* ends with a glance at questions of literary criticism: 'This introduction would not be complete without some mention of literary theory' (5). The phrase 'some mention' necessarily creates a certain feeling of uneasiness in the reader.

---

⁷ All notions of abstract calculative systems which we apply to the past and (!) to the future do not function for ancient times. E.g. January 1, 1101 - the first day of the 12th century in our counting - was St.Basil's feast 6609 in the Byzantine calendar counting, midway through a conventional year. On concepts of time in Byzantium see V. Grumel, *La chronologie* (Paris 1958) and for the Middle Ages in general D. J. Wilcox, *The Measure of Times Past. Pre-Newtonian Chronologies and the Rhetoric of Relative Time* (Chicago 1987).

⁸ We are far removed from having a history of Byzantine studies. For a different approach concerning the study of the Komnenian and Palaiologian works, see Agapitos, *Narrative Structure* 1-10 and *id.,* 'Byzantine Literature and Greek Philologists in the Nineteenth Century', ClMed 43 (1992) [forthcoming].

Beyond the mention of Gerard Genette's narratological study[9] and the haphazard references to Hans Robert Jauss, Wolfgang Iser and other critics, the book remains completely on the surface of the basic problem: can literary theory as developed after the Second World War contribute to the study of medieval literature, and if so, what is the way in which it may contribute? The random quotations from the works of famous critics, as will be shown often enough in the following pages, appear ultimately as an external modernization rather than as a result of an aesthetically developed eclecticism, revealing the author's lack of knowledge in the field of literary criticism.

---

[9] Quoted throughout the book with the date 1980, and no mention of the fact that the original French text was published in 1972. The full reference is G. Genette, 'Discours du récit. Essai de méthode', in: *id.*, *Figures iii* (Paris 1972) 65-282. Genette's study, which presents a narratological theory based almost exclusively on Proust's *A la recherche du temps perdu*, and which does not in the least purport to be a handbook of narratology, found both admirers and critics. As a result, Genette replied 11 years later in a shorter study, clarifying numerous points and adding new material (*Nouveau discours du récit* [Paris 1983], translated also into English by Jane E. Lewin [Ithaca, N.Y. 1988]). Of this Beaton makes no mention.

Chapter 1

The twelfth-century background

The author opens the first chapter of his study with a presentation of the background to the twelfth century. As he had already noted in his *Introduction*, he offers the battle at Manzikert in 1071 as the decisive turning point in the socio-cultural and national development of the Byzantine Empire. He suggests that because of the sudden loss of major areas of the Empire, the Byzantines found themselves in a situation where spoken language and state coincided in creating accidentally 'something very like a national identity' (8).

For one thing, words like 'sudden' and 'accidentally' cannot in anyway explain historical phenomena gestating over longer periods of time. Moreover, modern historians are not in full agreement that Manzikert was such an important 'break',[10] while the studies Beaton quotes are of a general nature and without proper documentation on this particular question.[11] We agree that the battle of Manzikert was a shock to its contemporaries, only the reasons for this shock are in our opinion not those suggested by Beaton. What disturbed Constantinopolitan society was the fact that the Roman Emperor had been captured by the barbarians, a tremendous loss of prestige for the State.[12] A number of points in the author's argumentation are contradicting each other. He considers the 12th century as a transitional period (identity crisis, rise of national feeling, unity of language), yet at the same time presents it as 'marked by the firm and stable rule of the Comnenian dynasty' where 'the intellectual "renaissance" of the eleventh century seems to have been checked' (9), obviously a case of *non sequitur* in his argument.

---

[10] See, for example, the cautious remarks by A. P. Kazhdan & A. W. Epstein, *Change in Byzantine Culture in the Eleventh and Twelfth Centuries* (Berkeley / Los Angeles / London 1985) 24f. and P. Lemerle, *Cinq études sur le xie siècle* (Paris 1977) 263-287 on economic, military and administrative questions.

[11] Beaton's division of Byzantine history seems based on that of Cyril Mango, *Byzantium. The empire of New Rome* (London 1980); he also refers to A. Bryer, 'The first encounter with the west, A.D.1050-1204', in: P. Whitting (ed.), *Byzantium: an Introduction* (Oxford 1981) 83-110; less easy, however, to understand is his reference to A. P. Kazhdan & S. Franklin, *Studies on Byzantine literature of the eleventh and twelfth centuries* (Cambridge 1984) 14 who do not agree with Mango.

[12] See the comments by Psellos, *Chron.* viib 22-23 (Impellizeri ii, 340-42), Bryennios i 17 (Gautier 117-119) and Attaleiates 160-166 (Bonn). On the question of this shock-effect see J. C. Cheynet, 'Mantzikert: un désastre militaire?', Byzantion 50 (1980) 410-438.

Furthermore, and this seems to us the most problematic point, the author equates in a schematic way the use of language as means of social intercourse and as a literary vehicle. There can be no question that the Empire was multilingual in its early period, multilingual in the sense that various nationalities spoke their respective mother-tongues within the confines of the State. But is there enough documentation to show that this situation had changed substantially by the 11th-12th centuries? At any rate, the distinction between spoken and literary language must be kept in mind constantly. Some examples may serve to illuminate this distinction and the peculiar Hellenocentricity of the Empire on the literary linguistic level.

The great Father of the Church Ephraim the Syrian lived and taught most of his life outside the confines of the Empire in the 4th century. He wrote only in Syriac: his works met with great admiration and success but in translated Greek versions. So far the use of Greek as a literary vehicle. On a stormy September night in 867 when the group of men who had murdered emperor Michael III, led by Basileios, were seeking entrance into the palace, one of them spoke to the keeper of keys in their native language - Persian (i.e. Armenian) - and they were admitted.[13] So far the use of a national language as a means for specific social purposes. In his remarkable *tour de force* of linguistic prowess Tzetzes claimed to be able to be a Scythian among Scythians, a Latin among Latins, but he does not distinguish between nationality and citizenship.[14] At a much later point, in his polemical dialogue against the Jews (1464), Georgios Scholarios (ca.1405-ca.1472) was writing: [the Christian speaks] 'But let us look at language. I too know Latin; yet, I do not say that I am Latin, since I do not believe in the way Latins do (and I shall explain later on in what they differ from us); while being as to my language a Hellene, I would never say that I am a Hellene, since I do not believe what Hellenes once believed; so I shall call myself by my faith.'[15] It becomes obvious from these totally random examples that a notion of national

---

[13] Theod. Melit. (Tafel) 176, 10-11, Leo Gram. (Bonn) 252, 5-8.

[14] See for this text H. Hunger, BZ 46 (1953) 302-307, now reprinted in his *Byzantinische Grundlagenforschung* (London 1973). Translation in Kazhdan & Epstein (see above n. 10) 259.

[15] Gen. Schol. *Ἔλεγχος τῆς ἰουδαικῆς νῦν πλάνης*, in Gennade Scholarios, *Oeuvres complétes* ed. par L. Petit - X. A. Sidéridès - M. Jugie, vol. 3 (Paris 1930) 253, 1-6. Naturally, the polemical nature of this work asks for a forceful presentation. There are other moments where the learned Patriarch connects positively Ἕλλην and γένος, see Th. N. Zeses, *Γεννάδιος Β΄ Σχολάριος. Βίος, συγγράμματα, διδασκαλία* [Ἀνάλεκτα Βλατάδων 30] (Thessaloniki 1980) 78-79, 440-441. On *ethnos*, nationality and Christendom in the 12th century cf. D.R.Reinsch, 'Ausländer und Byzantiner im Werk der Anna Komnene', Rechtshistorisches Journal 8 (1989) 257-274.

identity cannot be postulated, much less that of an identity crisis.[16] In this sense the author's proposition that periods of political stability secure artistic production and vice versa cannot be accepted to explain the 'sudden appearance' (10) of fictional literature. At any rate, as a general principle of cultural history it may not easily recommend itself to anyone living in the 20th century. We do, of course, have cases in Byzantine history where political events are understood as moments of crisis. To the Byzantines the explanation for such a crisis, however, lies almost exclusively in the realm of religion: it is God who punishes the sinners and God again who saves the repentant. A good example comes from the very 11th century, where the climate is full of tension. Ioannes Mauropous delivers around 1061 a speech against the ethical decay of the empire, sin being the root of evil.[17] Finally, the possible shift from a 'bureaucratic' to a more 'military' administration between the 11th and the 12th centuries does not change the essence of the government or of imperial ideology. Even if society accepts military education as important for the formation of a young man's character or the military virtues of the emperor are stressed to a higher degree,[18] no one ever doubted that 'Roman' imperial monarchy and administration was the only acceptable form of government.[19] For the Byzantines there is no alternative to the imperial system of the Empire. Thus, to superimpose a failure on their part to adapt to the changing world is to misunderstand the conservative concept of the citizens and their administrators.

In what sense can the appearance of the romance in the 12th century or the use of the vernacular idiom be considered a literary experiment? Various forms of 'fiction'

---

[16] The idea of a national identity is based on the results of R. Browning's studies on 12th century intellectual history as he succinctly formulated them in his *The Byzantine Empire* (London 1980) 146-147, after a substantial series of articles reprinted in his volume of collected studies (*Studies on Byzantine History, Literature and Education* [London 1977]). Beaton does not quote Browning, justifiably - one could add - because the two pages in *The Byzantine Empire* are undocumented and oversimplified. But then Browning's book is addressed to a broader public. Had Beaton looked at Browning's articles he would not have drawn such easy conclusions.

[17] *Johannis Euchaitorum metropolitae quae in codice vaticano graeco 676 supersunt.* Edd P. de Lagarde - J. Bollig [Abhandlungen der historisch-philologischen Klasse der königlichen Gesellschaft der Wissenschaften zu Göttingen 28] (Göttingen 1882) 165-178. See also A. Karpozelos, Συμβολή στη μελέτη του βίου και του έργου του Ιωάννη Μαυρόποδος [Δωδώνη, Παράρτημα 18] (Ioannina 1982) 156-160.

[18] See A. Kazhdan, 'The Aristocracy and the Imperial Ideal', in M.Angold (ed.), *The Byzantine Aristocracy ix to xiii Centuries* [BAR International Series 221] (Oxford 1984) 43-57 and id., 'Certain Traits of Imperial Propaganda in the Byzantine Empire from the Eighth to the Fifteenth Centuries' in: *Prédication et propagande au moyen âge. Islam, Byzance, Occident* (Paris 1983) 13-28.

[19] See, for example, the essay on monarchy by Theodoros Metochites in his *Miscellanea* (Müller-Kiesling [Leipzig 1821] 625-642).

literature did exist before 1100 (longer narratives like the *Barlaam and Joasaph* or *Syntipas*, satiric dialogue like the *Philopatris*, etc.) and one cannot talk of sudden appearances. The learned romances of the 12th century do not appear as disconnected from their surroundings as Beaton suggests. We do, of course, agree with Hans Robert Jauss' statement concerning the revival of past forms of literature[20] and Beaton's proposition (10-11) that such a revival could be seen here. But it is not so sudden, nor so astounding, if one looks at the whole development of scholarly and literary activities since the 10th century.

Beaton then turns to the question of language and its 'levels' in Byzantium. He presents us with the extremes of Anna Komnene's 'high atticist' diction and the vernacular idiom of the *Ptochoprodromika*:

> 'In each case, what is sought, whether fully consciously or not, is an identity for the writer and his public as 'Greek', which may replace or co-exist uneasily with his received identity as citizen of God's earthly kingdom. In the case of the high Atticist, such as Anna Komnini, the search is for the authentication of that identity in a past as remote, and therefore as authoritative, as that of the Bible; in the case of writers who experimented with the vernacular, of which the ones mentioned are only the most thoroughgoing examples, similar authentication is sought (usually playfully) in something shared as a lowest common denominator: the language of the street and the names of trades and utensils in the poems attributed to Prodromos, the common heritage of proverbial wisdom in Glykas' (11).

Nothing in this statement can be documented. What kind of identity does Komnene seek in her choice of a complex stylistic register? How can the language of the street be the common denominator between the author of the *Ptochoprodromika* and the emperor to whom the poems are addressed? And how does one explain, if one accepts the authorship of Theodoros Prodromos, the shifts in linguistic register, meter, diction and imagery

---

[20] The German critic, in a study entitled 'Literaturgeschichte als Provokation der Literaturwissenschaft' (originally his inaugural lecture at the University of Konstanz in 1969; reprinted in H. R. Jauss, *Literaturgeschichte als Provokation* [Frankfurt a.M. 1970] 144-207 (Beaton quotes only the English translation)) questioned the accepted historically linear (*qua* generic) approach of romantic and post-romantic German histories of literature, thus explaining a particular stillstand in literary analysis and in particular the analysis of medieval literature. He proposed a most interesting and quite workable theory of cyclical/interactive literary tradition, where (to put it roughly) an author receives older material in his work, hands it over to the reader, who in his turn valorizes it culturally and hands it over to another author, thus starting a new cycle (see also below p. 74).

between the 'Homeric' beggar poem to Anna Komnene (Hörandner no. xxxviii)[21], the 'koine' fifteen-syllable verse poem to Theodoros Stypiotes (Hörandner no. lxxi), the 'Maiuri' poem[22] and *Ptochoprodr.* iv? Where lies the authentication or search for identity here?

This brings us to the slippery ground of 'diglossia'.[23] If, for a moment, we accept the existence of three levels of style,[24] is the literary vernacular to be fitted there? Does the vernacular (and the definition of this vernacular idiom by itself poses problems) represent the 'low' level, of which Anna's text represents the 'high'? Surely, there is a gap between written and spoken language in the middle ages not only in the Latin West but also in the Arab East.[25] But if one really wants to be strict, does the vernacular give us an accurate picture of the spoken idiom of the 12th century? Especially after the studies of Alexiou on the *Ptochoprodromika* and Apostolopoulos on the *Kallimachos*[26] one should be careful in equating the vernacular with the spoken language of the time or the 'low' style.

Having concluded the section on language the author moves on to the question of 'Literacy, books and readers'. We are somewhat at a loss here: he presents in two pages a summary of other scholars' hypotheses without actually suggesting what is his own view. A major point emerges again: the notion of 'entertainment' literature, now enriched with the distinction between secular and ecclesiastical reading public. Can there really exist such a distinction for the Byzantines? When the Byzantines talked about secular and ecclesiastical they meant specifically pagan and Christian, and furthermore by pagan they meant the works of antiquity.[27] They did not distinguish their own works in these categories. Furthermore, lay readers did read Christian literature, just as ecclesiastics

---

[21] *Theodoros Prodromos. Historische Gedichte* [Wiener Byzantinistische Studien 11] (Wien 1974).

[22] The vernacular poem edited by A. Maiuri, BZ 23 (1920) 397-407.

[23] See the remarks by E. Kriaras, 'Ἡ διγλωσσία στα υστεροβυζαντινά γράμματα και η διαμόρφωση των αρχών της νεοελληνικής λογοτεχνίας', Βυζαντινά 8 (1976) 215-243 (reprinted in: *id.*, *Μεσαιωνικά μελετήματα. Γραμματεία και γλώσσα Β΄* [Thessaloniki 1988] 449-477).

[24] As developed by H. Hunger, 'Stilstufen in der Geschichtsschreibung des 12. Jahrhunderts: Anna Komnena und Michael Glykas', Byzantine Studies 5 (1978) 139-170 and Ihor Sevcenko, 'Levels of Style in Byzantine Prose', JÖB 31.1 (1981) 290-312. See also *id.*, 'Additional Remarks to the Report', JÖB 32.1 (1982) 220-229.

[25] See G. E. von Grunebaum, *Der Islam im Mittelalter* (Zürich-Stuttgart^3 1963) 11-19.

[26] Margaret Alexiou, 'The Poverty of Écriture and the Craft of Writing: Towards a Reappraisal of the Prodromic Poems', BMGS 10 (1986) 1-40 and Ph. Apostolopoulos, *La langue du roman byzantin 'Callimaque et Chrysorrhoé'* [Diss. Paris IV-Sorbonne 1972] (Athens 1984).

[27] See the remarks by F.Boulenger in his edition of Basileios' essay Πρὸς τοὺς νέους ὅπως ἂν ἐξ ἑλληνικῶν ὠφέλοιντο λόγων (Paris 1935) 16-23, the essay itself (for which see also the edition by Nigel G. Wilson [London 1976]) and Basileios' *ep.*135 (*Saint Basile, Lettres*. Texte établi et traduit par Y. Courtonne. Tome ii [Paris 1961] 49-51).

(churchmen and monks) read 'secular' works.[28]

Moreover, one should be very cautious when measuring popularity of a work by the number of surviving manuscripts, especially in the case of the romances; the vernacular works have all been preserved in post-Byzantine manuscripts. It is highly probable that a good deal of them were written in the West and destined for manuscript collectors there; they cannot be used as evidence for the actual Byzantine readership.[29] In fact, we know very little about Byzantine readers. We would warn, however, against drawing parallels from Hellenistic times and Late Antiquity where we seem to know more.[30] Beaton (15) suggesting a parallel with the Hellenistic world and the readers of the antique romances proposes that the romances were intended for silent reading by oneself - an idea based on a misunderstanding of a scene in Ach. Tat. i 6 where the hero is pretending to read but casts furtive glances at the heroine. As far as we can see there is nothing in the text that suggests that he is reading silently.[31] At this point it is also worth the while to point out that many of the extant manuscripts of the romances can be found in such small formats that it is almost certain that they were meant as a kind of pocketbook. Moreover, these manuscripts contain as the first text mostly some religious material which thus provides camouflage for the more mundane main contents of the books. Beaton claims with a reference to H.-G. Beck[32] that this need not be taken seriously, but anyone who cares to look up what Beck said will find this a gross misrepresentation. Beck, in fact, accepts the idea of a prayerbook cover for the love romance, but points out that this does not prove that the Church actively tried to suppress this type of literature.

The chapter ends with a discussion of the relations between East and West. Once again Beaton offers no conclusions on his own part, leaving the reader in uncertainty about the nature of the cultural interaction between East and West. One thing, though, that clearly emerges from his presentation is the complete lack of evidence concerning all movements of influence. We will not discuss here these generalizations, but leave detailed

---

[28] On these questions see now the comprehensive presentation by H. Hunger, *Schreiben und Lesen in Byzanz. Die byzantinische Buchkultur* [Beck's Archäologische Bibliothek] (München 1989) 125-136.

[29] On this and related questions see below pp. 66f, 100 and 104.

[30] See, for instance, the brief remarks by Tomas Hägg, *Den antike romanen* (Uppsala 1980) 106ff.

[31] Beaton used the Loeb edition by Gaselee who has partially mistranslated the passage, as Vilborg has pointed out in his commentary, *Achilles Tatius, Leucippe and Clitophon. A Commentary by* Ebbe Vilborg [Studia graeca et latina Gothoburgensia xv] [Acta Universitatis Gothoburgensis] (Stockholm 1962) 24.

[32] *Byzantinisches Erotikon* (München 1986) 165.

criticism for the respective chapters where the various works are analyzed.

Chapter 2

The literary tradition

Beaton attempts in this chapter to give a broad overview of Byzantine literature, based, as far as can be seen from the secondary works to which he refers, on a small number of modern books of a mostly general nature. It goes without saying that in order to discuss in a meaningful way the character of Byzantine literary tradition, it will not do to refer only to more popularizing accounts like Mango's *Byzantium*[33] nor to the admittedly much more specialised and detailed discussion by Hans-Georg Beck and Herbert Hunger in the *Byzantinisches Handbuch* series.[34] One result of the very superficial treatment in Beaton is the idea presented (19) of a literature of 'entertainment' in Byzantium (derived, it would seem, from Beck[35]) an idea which imports a doubtful notion into the Byzantine world.[36]

Of central importance to any understanding of Byzantine literature and literary tradition is the rhetorical nature of all texts produced in Byzantium. Rhetoric permeats the whole of literature, irrespective of contents and scope; in order to understand the workings of Byzantine rhetoric it is imperative to have a clear idea of both Byzantine education and the rhetorical tradition. Beaton concentrates on Hermogenes and Aphthonios, fair enough, it might be held, since these authors were of paramount importance within the whole system as it came to be practised in Byzantium. However, nothing is said about

---

[33] For full details see n. 11 above.

[34] H.-G.Beck, *Geschichte der byzantinischen Volksliteratur* [Byzantinisches Handbuch 2.3] (München 1971); Herbert Hunger, *Die hochsprachliche profane Literatur der Byzantiner i-ii* [Byzantinisches Handbuch 5.1-2] (München 1978). In fact, the *Byzantinisches Handbuch* is not some independent series, as Beaton suggests, but section xii in the famous Munich *Handbuch der Altertumswissenschaft*.

[35] 'Der Leserkreis der byzantinischen 'Volksliteratur' im Licht der handschriftlichen Überlieferung', in: *Byzantine Books and Bookmen*. Dumbarton Oaks Colloquium 1971 (Dumbarton Oaks, Washington D.C. 1975) 55.

[36] The whole problem of the literary public in Byzantium needs a thorough investigation before we can deal with such problems as whether one can speak of 'literature of entertainment' at all, and in what sense it is possible to speak of entertainment. The parallel to modern literature of entertainment (and even to mass media) and *Trivialliteratur* is found very often, but is no less objectionable.

other writers or the development from the Second Sophistic until the 12th century,[37] and Beaton is excessively preoccupied with Nikephoros Basilakes, as if this author's *Progymnasmata* could be regarded - as Beaton more or less implies - as a source for the romance.[38] It is extremely doubtful whether these texts can be thought of as sources at all; examples of the type of rhetorical models, yes, but not as sources. Beaton clearly regards Basilakes as a formative influence on Makrembolites, with no better argument than that Basilakes shares with Makrembolites the 'device of using an unattributed first-person narration' (23). Somewhat self-defeatingly, Beaton adds that this device is traditional to these exercises. So, if relevant at all, why not regard the whole of this tradition as the background for Makrembolites' technique?

Beaton seems to find it significant that Basilakes' διηγήματα often have a headline τὰ κατὰ ... as if this had something to do with the titles of the late antique romances. This is a standard expression, also to be found in Nikolaos' *Progymnasmata* in his sections on *refutatio* and *confirmatio*.[39] There are also some other slightly embarrassing statements here. Beaton (24) says (in connection with Basil. *progymn.* vii 26) that the garden-allegory of love as we find it in the *Roman de la Rose* in the West, is more limited in the medieval Greek romance, and refers in a general way to Littlewood's 'Romantic Paradises' for confirmation.[40] As far as we can see, Littlewood nowhere says so, the impression one gets from his analysis is rather that the garden imagery of love can be found prominently in all of the romances.[41]

Discussing the *ekphrasis*, Beaton notes (25) that 'it is remarkable how many Byzantine *ekphraseis* are either descriptions of works of art, or describe people and things as if they were works of art'. Now, as noted by Hunger, there are no *ekphraseis* of

---

[37] The best, but still not exhaustive account of the whole field is in Hunger, *Die hochsprachliche profane Literatur* i, 92-120; see also G. Kennedy, *Greek Rhetoric under Christian Emperors* (Princeton, N.J. 1983).

[38] Basilakes is one of the few Byzantine rhetoricians that can be found in a modern, though badly executed, edition: A. Pignani, *Nicephoro Basilace. Progimnasmi e monodie* [Byzantina et Neo-Hellenica Neapolitana. Collana di studi e testi 10] (Napoli 1983). It appears from D. R. Reinsch's substantial review in BZ 80 (1987) 89-91 that a revised version is needed. For most of the other authors and the commentaries we have to go back to the old and mostly unreliable collections in Spengel and Walz.

[39] C. Walz, *Rhetores graeci* vol.i, 284-319.

[40] A. R. Littlewood, 'Romantic paradises: the rôle of the garden in the Byzantine romance', BMGS 5 (1979) 95-114.

[41] Also, it seems to have escaped Beaton that Basil. *progymn.* vii 27 ('What Hades would say on Lazarus being raised from the dead') probably took its inspiration from Romanos' Anastasis-kontakia and not from a combination of antique and biblical traditions. See Hunger, *Die hochsprachliche profane Literatur* i 113.

nature at all;[42] the reason why descriptions of people tend to be in terms of works of art is obviously very simple, namely that works of art constituted a common and easily understood frame of reference (cf. below p. 41). Moreover, it should be noted that while it is true that works of art are praised in *ekphraseis* for their artifice, it is equally true that they are also praised for their likeness to life. For instance, the description of Priamos' throne in the *Byz. Iliad* 56ff emphasizes that the figures look as if they were alive and real, while there is nothing here about an artificer-poet:

        πέντε πουλιὰ ἐπέτουντα ἀπάνω εἰς τὸν θρόνον
        ἐκεῖ ὁποῦ ἐκάθητον Πρίαμος βασιλεύς τε.
        νὰ ἔλεγες ὡς ζωντανὰ καθολικὰ ὑπάρχουν,
        τρέχουσιν ἐκ τοῦ στόματος ἐκείνων τῶν πουλίων
60   νερὸ καὶ ἀποδίδουσιν εἰς ἀργυρὲς λεκάνες.
        ἀγάλματα πανέγλυπτα γῦρον τοῦ παλατίου
        τὸ μὲν νὰ παίζη μουσικόν, τὸ δὲ νὰ παίζη λύραν
        ἄλλο νὰ παίζη ἔντεχνον καλάμιν μετὰ πόθου.
        φωνὲς αἰσθήσεως σαρκὸς νὰ ἔλεγες ὅτ' ἦταν.[43]

Similar are the references in the *Achilleid* **N** 790 and **L** 527. Moreover, the point that these works of art must be the work of God emphasizes that they are lifelike.[44]

    The main problem of this section, however, is that Beaton does not really manage to give the reader an idea of the pervasive influence of Byzantine rhetoric, nor, by his basing himself on the handbooks of the Second Sophistic, does he get further than the rhetorical *topoi*. For a much more in-depth study one would have to analyze the texts of the romances from a stylistic point of view, using the tools offered by Byzantine rhetoric itself.[45]

    The following section in this chapter on realism and the individual is somewhat embarrassing. Beaton seems to equate developments in east and west (25). We do not feel

---

[42] *Op.cit.* i 170-188.

[43] In line 64 we have followed D. Dedes and R. Lavagnini in their interpretation of the MS.

[44] Beaton 145 claims that the use of the word ἀχειροποίητα (ἀγάλματα [this is a conjecture by Hesseling]) at **N** 794 might well have seemed risqué, and in his note 5 on p. 230 he says that the epithet is attributed to the deity in Byzantine texts which is definitely not true; it is used about things made by the deity. In fact, since the word was used about icons, there is nothing remarkable in its use here. By the way, in vernacular texts it is only found here and in one other passage where it is used about the church, see Kriaras, *Λεξικό* s.v.

[45] For such an approach, see Agapitos, *Narrative Structure* 141ff, where the narrative sequence of the *Kallimachos*, *Belthandros* and *Livistros* is analysed on the basis of rhetorical techniques as understood by the Byzantines. See also P. A. Agapitos, 'Michael Italikos, Klage auf den Tod seines Rebhuhns', BZ 82 (1989) 59-68.

confident in judging how far one can speak of 'innovation' in Western literature of the 11th and 12th centuries, nor whether it is true that one can see there 'the appearance of the author as an individual in his text', and find 'a new kind of reference in literary texts to the contingent world'. What we can say is that Beaton does not even attempt to argue for such developments in Byzantium, and as far as we know there is no evidence at all. Individualism and realism have no place in a Byzantine context, and the reader can see from Beaton's discussion in note 11 to this section that he has not really defined his terms.[46] He seems to move from the individual author to the individual character. Even if the justification of this is granted - which we doubt - it is difficult to see what evidence he has for his further assertion that 'the heroes and heroines of the medieval romance represent generalizations of the self' (26).

---

[46] His reference to Kazhdan & Franklin, *op. cit.* [see above n.11] 188 does not prove his case. For a discussion of the term 'realism' we should point to René Wellek's sober analysis 'The Concept of Realism in Literary Scholarship', Neophilologus 44 (1960) 1-20, reprinted in his collection of essays *Concepts of Criticism* (Yale 1963) 222-255.

Chapter 3

The 'proto-romance', *Digenis Akritis*

In the first section on the 'Precursors of the Romance' Beaton argues that the revival of the romance in the 12th century should be seen in the light of the break he finds with the battle at Manzikert, on which we commented above pp. 12 and 15. He believes that 'it is impossible not to see the revival of the romance in the twelfth century in terms of an increasing secularisation and the search for a new identity among Byzantine literati in the generations that came after Manzikert' (28). As we shall see, he also explains the genesis of the *Digenis* in this way. He is therefore at pains to play down the existence of fictional narrative in Byzantium before that date. He agrees, however, that written narrative can be found both in historiography and hagiography, but he claims that 'no emancipation of narrative discourse as an autonomous genre is *possible*' (27, our emphasis). To say the least, this is a highly modernistic statement; in fact, it is difficult to see what it could possibly mean in our context. The same goes for his further remark that the fictional narrative that indeed can be found at this time (translations from oriental literature, the Alexander story etc.) 'never quite establishes itself as a self-conscious literary genre' (28). As already pointed out, to speak of the self-consciousness of a literary genre in Byzantium is to our mind totally out of the question. We accept the conscious use of literary forms in the Middle Ages but point out that form and genre are distinct categories. The reason for these extraordinary statements (he also speaks here of an experimental secular literature in the 12th century [28]) is to exaggerate the 'break with the past' in the proto-romance of *Digenis*, and to downplay the significance of the fact that, as he himself has to admit, we do have a more or less unbroken narrative tradition in hagiography and in the fables, in the Alexander stories and in the oriental material. But though he has to admit as much, he emphasizes that saints' lives cease to be written altogether, and finds it striking that Prodromos is the last to write an original saint's life, and one of the first to write a medieval Greek romance.[47] Further he states (*ibid.*) that this narrative fiction still is the literature of the educated, whereas we have to wait until the 14th and 15th centuries for a popular form of this narrative tradition. The didactic function of much of this literature is taken

---

[47] The reference at this point in Beaton to Hörandner's edition of Prodromos (see above n. 21) p. 45 is misleading. There is nothing there to support the statement.

to speak against Beck's inclusion of it in his *Volksliteratur*. There is nowhere in Beaton a clear definition of what he means by 'popular'; one would think that such texts as saints' lives, Aesop's fables and *Syntipas* would qualify as popular literature, even if the language is not in any way 'modern Greek'. Ultimately, for Beaton 'popular' means 'vernacular' and nothing more.[48]

Finally, as for the lack of 'interaction' between historiography and its 'fictional counterpart in the romance' (apart from the dubious question of what such terms are supposed to mean in a Byzantine context), Beaton only reluctantly recognizes that there are some outstanding cases of Byzantine historiography taking on stories of a nature remarkably similar to the romances. Similarly, biographical writings are in themselves a combination between history and 'romantic' material. Plutarch is a classic case and at the same time the classical model for Byzantine literati. Historiography of the 10th century onwards in particular owes quite a lot to biographical/romantic typology. Works like Psellos' *Chronographia*, Bryennios' *Hyle historias* and Anna Komnene's *Alexias* are excellent examples of this new type of historiography. As for hagiography, the connection from Antiquity between Christian *apocrypha* and romance is well known, and the rhetorical typology in saints' lives is difficult to separate from secular descriptions. Beaton, however, shows his lack of familiarity with Byzantine rhetorics by implying that the *basilikos logos* is the prescription for formal narratives of praise (it is, of course, used for praise of the emperor only), and still worse, that the heroes and heroines of romances and saints' lives are depicted according to the rules for the *basilikos logos* (27).[49]

The discussion of the *Digenis* is marred by on one hand the failure to differentiate

---

[48] Behind Beaton's understanding of 'popular' seem to lie the ideas put forward by H.-G. Beck in his 'Leserkreis' (cf. above n. 35) where he tried to show that there is a clear distinction in the manuscript tradition between the 'educated' literature and the 'popular': the 12th century romances can mostly be found either together or in the company of traditional classical and Byzantine learned literature in the MSS, whereas the 'popular', the more or less vernacular texts appear in the 14th and 15th centuries and are only found together with other popular texts. But for one thing this, if true, cannot be taken to mean that Prodromos and the other 12th century romance writers were not 'popular' in terms of being attractive for the reading public, nor is it wholly legitimate to draw conclusions from the state of the MSS as they are found today. Some of these MSS have been rebound, and we have absolutely no means of certifying why for instance the texts in such MSS as *Par. gr.* 2898 (*Chronicle of The Morea, Theseid*), British Museum *Add.* 8241 (*Florios, Achilleid*) and Naples iii. B. 27 (*Achilleid, Belisarios*) were bound together. The reason might simply be 16th century notions about 'vulgar' texts.

[49] As often in Beaton's book the explanation can be found in his source. He refers here to Cyril Mango, *Byzantium. The Empire of New Rome* (London 1980) 247-248 where Mango on the basis of Menander Rhetor outlines the prescriptions for the *basilikos logos* and claims that this schema *mutatis mutandis* was used in celebrating Christian saints, a far from proven hypothesis.

between the biographical plot of the life of one man and the romances, on the other hand by the insistence on an 'original' *Digenis*. Beaton admits, as everyone must, that the differences between the two oldest manuscript versions, **E** and **G**,[50] are so great that each version has to be discussed separately; still, he rejects the idea that the two versions might be independent realizations of the same basic story material. He does so by referring in note 11 on p. 215 to St. Alexiou's 1985 edition of the Escorial version pp. 29-30 where no argument can be found to strengthen his claim that Alexiou 'conclusively' has disproved this possibility ('γιὰ μᾶς εἶναι αὐτονόητο' says Alexiou p. 30), which we would argue can be supported from the state of affairs regarding the *Achilleid* and the *Livistros*, both of which texts have been transmitted in mutually incompatible versions.

Beaton also claims that the Escorial version, or one very like it, was already well known in Constantinople by the second half of the 12th century. Again, St. Alexiou (pp. 121-123) is referred to, and again we are confronted with no argument. It is, to say the least, not very accurate to tell the reader (33) that there is good evidence for this *terminus ante*. The result of this insistence on an original version is that Beaton operates with interpolations and omissions by the scribe (or the redactor) of the **E** version.

The language of the **E** version is a notorious problem. Beaton more or less gives up reaching a solution by pointing to the various difficulties and the mutually exclusive theories put forward to explain the linguistic amalgam. Two factors, however, brought into the picture are of a dubious nature. One is the possible effects of the vagaries of the manuscript tradition. But we have absolutely no idea of whether there is any manuscript tradition behind the Escorial manuscript and if so how many stages we are removed from the 'original' version (irrespective of whether this is regarded as the original *Digenis*). The other is the Cretan influence. It is stated, once again with reference to St. Alexiou, that the MS seems to have been copied in Crete, and that intrusions from the Cretan linguistic idiom have been identified in the text. The reader will by now have guessed that nothing on this can be found in Alexiou, who takes it for granted that the scribe was a

---

[50] For the manuscript **E** see G. De Andrés, *Catálogo de los códices griegos de la Real Biblioteca de El Escorial* iii (Madrid 1967) 106-109, and Agapitos, *Narrative Structure* 29-31 for the most updated references to further literature and for **G** see L. Politis, 'L'épopée byzantine de Digenis Akritas', *Atti del convegno internazionale sul tema: La poesia epica e la sua formazione* [Accademia Nazionale dei Lincei 357] (Roma 1970) Quaderno no. 139, 553-554 with the important modification of the accepted date; Politis would assign the MS to some time between the second half of the 13th century and the beginning of the 14th. It would seem, though, that also **G** badly needs a full modern description and codicological analysis. There is nothing in Trapp's edition.

Cretan.[51] The dialect intrusions were argued by Xanthoudidis[52] whose results should be reconsidered before they are accepted today. It has become more and more difficult, if not to say impossible to pin-point modern Greek dialectal elements in Byzantine vernacular texts. Older scholars were far more ready to do this than is prudent today. And as far as we know there is no codicological information available to settle the question of the provenance of the manuscript.[53]

Beaton does not deal with the socalled **Z** version since he accepts (215 n.13) Michael Jeffreys' ingenious demonstration[54] that the **Z** version was based on no more than what we have in **E** and **G**, and that moreover one of the two sources for **Z** was the actual MS **E**. It appears that **Z**, in fact, used the very MS **E** in its present acephalic state. The loss of three folios at the beginning of the *Digenis* and the probably simultaneous loss of a

---

[51] Beaton refers to Alexiou p. 8 and 17. On p. 8 the scribe is simply mentioned as a Cretan, whereas there is nothing on p. 17. According to Beaton Alexiou on these pages is also supposed to have shown that the text was influenced by the Cretan dialect of the scribe. There is nothing at all about this.

[52] Χριστιανική Κρήτη 1 (1913) 523f. Xanthoudidis' arguments were accepted by Gareth Morgan, 'Cretan Poetry: Sources and Inspiration', Κρητικά χρονικά 14 (1960) 44-68, especially 46-48, who is quoted with approval by E. M. and M. J. Jeffreys, 'The Style of Byzantine Popular Poetry: Recent Work', in: *Okeanos*. Essays presented to Ihor Ševčenko, Harvard Ukrainian Studies 7 (1983) 312. But Kyriakidis in his report at the Munich 1958 congress questioned the Cretan influence, 'Forschungsbericht zum Akritas-Epos', *Berichte zum XI. Internationalen Byzantinistenkongress II.2* (München 1958) 18. Recently, there has been an attempt by I.K.Promponas, Ακριτικά Α´ (Athens 1985) to find a Pontic dialectal substratum in version **E**, which is also difficult to accept. That there are elements of formulaic composition, as Promponas has seen, is quite another story (see the review of Promponas' study by Alexiou, Ελληνικά 39 [1988] 189-195). At any rate, the changing opinion from Cretan to Pontic shows that in reality it is almost impossible to determine modern Greek dialectal elements in medieval vernacular texts.

[53] In view of the importance of this manuscript and the number of scholars who have dealt with it, it is shocking to see that it is still possible to doubt basic facts or their interpretation, see St. Alexiou's false arguments from the watermarks against a later date than the middle of the 15th century, p. 16 note 5. G. De Andrés, *Catálogo* 108 gives as the only watermark in the vernacular part of the MS ff. 22-213 'Briquet n.11194 var. sim.' Now, Briq. n.11194 is found in 1485, but as far as we know no one has ever been able to get nearer than this to the actual watermark in these folios, and thus we cannot be absolutely certain of the date. L. Politis, 'L'épopée' 554 n.11) gives (from De Andrés' catalogue) 'pareille à Briquet no. 11194' as the watermark found in the MS and thus keeps the all-important qualification ('pareille à') which Alexiou in his reference to Politis omits. Alexiou just gives the Briquet number. It should be emphasized, however, that de Andrés' date (middle of 15th century) which has been accepted without further ado by most scholars is based on the false theory that the MS is an unity (including the theological texts at the beginning and end of the MS) whereas it is pretty obvious from De Andrés' own analysis that ff. 22-213 should be treated as a separate whole. Politis (*ibid.*) rightly pointed out that de Andrés' date should be more precise. He has been followed (though without reference) by E. D. Kakoulidi, Ελληνικά 24 (1971) 271 n.1.

[54] Δωδώνη 4 (1975) 163-201, reprinted in *Popular Literature in late Byzantium* (London 1983).

whole gathering at the end of *Livistros* point to a situation where the MS had been taken apart, most likely in order to be rebound. There is no numbering of gatherings in the MS but the original part containing the vernacular texts seems to have been executed as a whole.[55] It should be investigated whether the rebinding that obviously created the present chaos in the MS took place when the MS had already come to Spain; that is, whether the present binding is Italian or Spanish. Also one should consider the less likely possibility that the *Livistros* and the *Digenis* may have circulated as single books, as was proposed by H.-G. Beck in the case of the texts in the Vienna MS *theol. gr.* 244.[56]

The discussion of the **G** version suffers from the same basic misconceptions, and we are even introduced to our old friend, the unfortunate 'monastic copyist' (39) invoked to take the blame for the authorial comments on the action as well as the prologue.[57] Some other disquieting features appear here in Beaton's analysis. There are gross errors both in the Greek texts (they might be looked upon as printers' errors, of course) and in the translations of the Greek.[58]

Beaton claims (36) that the change into first-person narrative in the **G** version at the beginning of Book v 'has been, surely rightly, identified as an imitation of the *Odyssey*'(referring to Trapp's edition pp. 69-70[59]) and he then goes on to draw conclusions from this about the general structure of the whole original poem, arguing that the Maximou episode,[60] which has been doubted as part of the original poem, makes sense. Now, first of all, the reference to Trapp is not wholly justified, for what Trapp says there (on p. 70) is not that the *Digenis* here imitates the *Odyssey*, but that the first-person narrative is 'vergleichbar'. No more and no less. Then one may notice that Beaton (43) contradicts himself by saying that there is no reason to believe that the author of **G**

---

[55] The composition of the MS in its original state is set forth with great acumen by Chatzigiakoumis, Μεσαιωνικά κείμενα 71-75.

[56] 'Leserkreis' 67. It stands to reason that this should be investigated in more detail. Meanwhile we have to wait for the second volume of the new Vienna catalogue of the *theologici graeci* prepared by Herbert Hunger and Ernst Gamillscheg. See H. Schreiner, 'Die zeitliche Aufeinanderfolge der im Cod. Vindob. Theol. Gr. 244 überlieferten Texte des Imberios, des Belisar und des Florios, und ihr Schreiber', BZ 55 (1962) 213-223, and our corrections about the scribes of **V** below n. 233.

[57] On these asides see now P. Odorico, 'La sapienza del Digenis. Materiali per lo studio dei *loci similes* nella recensione di Grottaferrata', Byzantion 59 (1989) 137-163.

[58] For instance, on p. 35 **G** iv 970 ἄλλα μέρη ἱκανά is rendered as 'other well-defended places'. In line 967 συναπέτεινε is an error for συναπέκτεινε.

[59] Erich Trapp, *Digenes Akrites. Synoptische Ausgabe der ältesten Versionen* [Wiener Byzantinistische Studien 8] (Wien 1971).

[60] We have been unable to explain to ourselves why Beaton translates **G** vi 837 (Digenis speaking about his murder of Maximou) ταύτην .... ἀνηλεῶς ἀνεῖλον 'I pitilessly obliterated her'.

or of its original knew the Homeric poems directly. And on the next page (44) the change to first-person narrative becomes 'an allusion to the story, not necessarily to the text, of the *Odyssey*.'

One may agree with the remarks (37) about the coherence in the **G** version, but we certainly disagree with Beaton's claims about the passage **G** iv 241-253 which leads abruptly from Digenis' hunting adventures to his abduction of the girl. Beaton finds here that 'the imagery subtly but unmistakably points to a newly acquired sexuality'. We admit not being able to see anything but Digenis as the usual male sexual object in the Byzantine romance. There is not a word here about a 'newly' acquired sexuality; the passage simply does not bring this out, and Beaton does not quote anything to prove his point. What this 'abrupt' transition shows is that the basic story and the logic of the plot is so well known to the audience that no further explanation is needed.[61] It would seem that in **E** Digenis may have been represented as having met the girl already, if it is correct that there is a lacuna in **E** between 791 and 792 in which such a meeting may have been described. At least **E** 835 speaks of the girl as if she had been mentioned already.

The remarks on the metre in the **G** version, where Beaton finds that the metrical practice with a dactylic/anapaestic rhythm in the second half of the verse cutting across the basic iambic pattern is a deliberate choice, an 'attempt to reproduce in accentual terms the metrical pattern with which the Homeric hexameter regularly ends' (39) are highly doubtful, to say the least. Beaton overlooks not only the insurmountable difference between accentual and quantitative metre, but also the very characteristics of the political verse. Does he imply that each 'long' element in the iambic rhythm was invariably stressed?[62]

Beaton comes finally to the question of the language of **G** (39). He rightly rejects the subjective view of St. Alexiou who regarded it as 'solecist', and finds that **G** shows a less inconsistent language than does **E** (40). However, as he says, 'consistency is no guarantee of authenticity' and concludes by pointing out, as he must, that both witnesses to the original *Digenis* may have been the product of linguistic transposition, and that each text contains a significant number of superior readings as well as of linguistic

---

[61] In which case there is a parallel in the narrative technique of the Oxford *Achilleid*, see O.L.Smith, 'Notes on the Byzantine Achilleid. The Oxford Version', ClMed 39 (1988) 259ff.

[62] Besides P. Maas, 'Der byzantinische Zwölfsilber', BZ 12 (1903) 272-323 and id., 'Metrische Akklamationen der Byzantiner' BZ 21 (1912) 28-51 (both articles have been reprinted in Maas' *Kleine Schriften* herausgegeben von Wolgang Buchwald [München 1973] 242-288, 393-418), one can profit from the short but dense presentation by L. Politis, Νεοελληνική (βυζαντινή καί νεωτέρα) μετρική, Μεγάλη Ἑλληνικὴ Ἐγκυκλοπαίδεια 17 (1931) 101-103. See also the collection of essays on Byzantine and Modern Greek metrics in Μαντατοφόρος 32 (1990) with further bibliography.

awkwardnesses. If this is so, we would emphasize, the whole idea of an original *Digenis* disappears. We have no objection to that conclusion, but surely Beaton should have seen that his own analysis leads to results that he himself contradicts elsewhere, and especially in the following section (40-48) where he attempts to say something about the original *Digenis*. He first deals with the sources of the original poem, and has some difficulty in making up his mind about the oral material. It follows from his view of the two versions that they are not independent oral realizations of a common story, so he does not admit that the sources of the original poem were exclusively oral. Unfortunately, there is nothing to go upon. Beaton does not succeed in proving or even suggesting any specific literary source for the original poem. Vague similarities there are, but not of a kind so as to support Beaton's confident statement that 'given that these literary sources underlie both extant versions of our text ... what can we infer about the nature of the original poem?' (44). We have already mentioned the 'Homeric' influence in **G** claimed by Beaton, and the other examples are not of better quality. To argue that the inclusion of *ekphraseis* in both **E** and **G** shows that the original poem is influenced by the Hellenistic romances will not convince anyone conversant with Byzantine literature of any age.

Worse is to follow, and we are sorry to say that the subsequent speculations on the nature of the original poem are totally unfounded. Beaton regards the poem as an attempt 'to graft a self-consciously literary treatment upon material derived from oral tradition in the vernacular' (44) and that this composite of popular and learned tradition is symbolized in the name 'Digenis' which refers to the programmatic intentions of the text itself. This is then taken still further, that the original poem followed the language and style of the sources it adopted for different parts of the narration. Prodromos in his vernacular poems is mentioned as a parallel, but this is a wholly different matter, since the various registers employed and the changes in style and language in Prodromos make sense as literary and artistic procedures, the linguistic amalgam in the original *Digenis* (to judge from **E** and **G** according to Beaton) does not.

As for the date of the original poem Beaton (46) refers to Michael Angold's proposal that the poem was composed in Constantinople,[63] but would put the date with St. Alexiou to the first decade of the 12th century. Then Beaton makes the further claim that an element of conscious antiquarianism or nostalgia enters into the original composition, since the poem deals with oral tales of the Eastern frontier which for several hundred years must have existed beneath the notice of literature. To account for such antiquarianism and nostalgia Beaton returns to his panacean idea of Manzikert and the

---

[63] N. Oikonomides also put forward this idea in 'L' "Epopée" de Digénis et la frontière orientale de Byzance aux Xe et XIe siècles', Travaux & Mémoires 7 (1979) 397.

'drastic change of attitude'. In this way the *Digenis* becomes comparable to the post-1922 literature about Asia Minor.[64] In the *Digenis*, the author of the original poem wanted to preserve the lost traditions by conferring upon them the immortality of literary expression. Unfortunately all this is pure speculation, based on no evidence but implying some serious misconceptions about Byzantine literature.

As for the genre of the poem Beaton tries to steer a middle course between the 'national epic' idea and the 'romance'. In fact, he regards the poem as something in-between, that it consciously (once again this dangerous word, which he never explains) initiates a movement from oral epic to heroic ballad. As far as we can see we have to acquiesce in the fact that the poem is *sui generis*, it is a genre of its own; at least its biographical plot makes it a wholly different thing in comparison with the romances.[65]

---

[64] Of course, we are not implying that Beaton would equate such different literatures and contexts, but his reference to the post-1922 Modern Greek literature nicely illustrates the difference between literature with and without self-consciousness.

[65] On the relation of *Digenis*' biographical plot and historiography see A. Markopoulos, 'Ο Διγενής Ακρίτης και η βυζαντινή χρονογραφία. Μία πρώτη προσέγγιση', Αριάδνη 5 (1989) 165-171.

Chapter 4

The renaissance of a genre

An indispensable tool of the hermeneutic method is the detailed analysis of the evidence at hand, in the case of literary criticism the analysis of the available texts on all their semantic levels. This analytical approach presupposes first the examination of previous theories and second the establishing of a basis as firm as possible on which the existing evidence is placed. What is not permissible is to press the existing evidence into a rigid concept which has been chosen *a priori* by the critic. This is exactly what Beaton offers the reader in Chapter 4: on the basis of a superficial study of the ancient novel which consists in assembling a 'collage'-sort of theory out of some recent works, he sets up a frame to interpret the reemergence of the novel in the 12th century. This frame is based solely on one idea and one idea alone: the notion of individual salvation which the characters of the respective text seek within the confines of the story. This salvation-motif is explained for the ancient romances through the concept of the 'age of anxiety',[66] and this is projected on the Byzantine world of the 11th and 12th centuries which according to Beaton is suffering from an identity 'Angst' following the battle of Manzikert. The only difference between the late antique and medieval situations is a nice chiastic inversion: whereas in the former we have Christianity taking over the function of salvation and thus bringing about the end of the novel, in the Komnenian age we have a revival of pagan philosophy leading to the reappearance of the novel which now takes over the function of salvation in a secular, non-Christian context. This schema is convenient but presupposes a series of theoretical constructs which are highly contestable.

For one thing, to generalize the essence of the ancient novel as 'the quest of the solitary individual for salvation in a violent and irrational world ruled (actually or apparently) by Chance (τύχη), through the love of another in its own likeness' (50), is to equate the novel with exactly those interpretations of a religious character which

---

[66] This idea was developed by E. R. Dodds in his famous Sather Classical Lectures (*The Greeks and the Irrational* [Berkeley 1951]) and later refined in his *Pagan and Christian in an Age of Anxiety* (Cambridge 1965). Beaton characteristically refers to the 'age of anxiety' (50) as if the idea was developed by E. L. Bowie in his discussion of the ancient romances in *The Cambridge History of Classical Literature* vol.I (Cambridge 1985) 687-688, which of course gives a completely distorted picture of modern scholarly studies.

Beaton himself rejects.[67] Furthermore, he bases the Byzantine anxiety on the Manzikert-syndrome which - as we have pointed out several times already - cannot be so readily accepted. As for the use of pagan philosophy and the 'secularization' of the State, we would recommend the greatest caution. For one thing, Byzantine philosophy is not in any way separate from the educationally accepted reception of Plato, Aristotle and their late antique commentators. To talk about the revival of pagan philosophy as a self-conscious, distinct discipline is highly dubious.[68] Psellos, for example, used his knowledge of sources to collect 'pagan' material in exactly the same way as he did for his theological treatises.[69] Similarly, Italos used philosophical syllogisms to reach conclusions about theological affairs. Moreover, the attack by an individual scholar on his rival with the accusation of paganism is a feature common also in earlier times in Byzantium (Niketas David Paphlagon accusing Photios[70] or Arethas attacking Leo Choirosphaktes[71]) and not peculiar to a rise of pagan philosophy in the 12th century. In the case of Italos it is connected with specific political purposes of the governing regime; it is indicative that in the 12th century Italos continued to be viewed as an uncultivated boorish foreigner, while Psellos was not.[72]

Beyond that, what does the expression 'rise of secular literature' (51) mean for 12th century Byzantium? Not very much, as far as we are concerned, because Beaton equates secular with the romances, a totally unacceptable equation. The salvation-motif which Beaton extracts from all the texts (though in fact it is impossible to do so) and superimposes on all literature, must be rethought and defined more clearly for individual works.

Having proposed his point of view ('the key to this revival of fiction and the

---

[67] He mentions Karl Kerenyí but fails to refer to the work of Reinhold Merkelbach, *Roman und Mysterium in der Antike* (München/Berlin 1962).

[68] On the whole issue see B.Tatakis, *Βυζαντινή φιλοσοφία* (Athens^4 1977).

[69] See the instructive *apparatus fontium* in the new volumes of the Teubner Psellos edition (Michael Psellos, *Theologica* vol. i ed. P. Gautier [Leipzig 1989] and *id.*, *Philosophica minora* vol. ii ed. D. J. O'Meara [Leipzig 1989]). On Psellos' general method of dealing with his sources see R. Volk, *Der medizinische Inhalt der Schriften des Michael Psellos* [Miscellanea Byzantina Monacensia 32] (München 1990) 449-459.

[70] Paphlagon in his *Life of Patriarch Ignatios*, PG 105, col. 528B-C; see also the anti-Photian anecdotal material in Ps.-Sym. 28-36 (Theoph. Cont. 668-674 Bonn).

[71] Arethas, *Scripta minora* ed. L.G.Westerink I (Lipsiae 1968) 200-212.

[72] In the anonymous satirical dialogue *Timarion* (editions by R.Romano [Napoli 1974] and M.D.MacLeod [*Luciani opera* iv (Oxford 1987) 432-470]); translation by B.Baldwin (Detroit 1984). On Psellos being read in the 12th century, see K. Snipes, 'The *Chronographia* of Michael Psellos and the Textual Tradition and Transmission of the Byzantine Historians of the Eleventh and Twelfth Centuries', Zbornik Radova 27/28 (1989) 43-62.

beginning in the east of its modern development, must be sought in *what the Byzantine authors saw in the works they chose to imitate*' [50]) he proceeds to present five thematic elements (partly abstract concepts, partly motifs, partly stylistic devices) found in the ancient novels 'which are repeated or even exaggerated by its Byzantine successors; some of which, as we shall see, acquire radically new meanings by being repeated in the twelfth century' (51).

The first of these elements concerns 'the past'. Beaton presents first the system of allusions used both by late antique and Byzantine authors. However, the allusion to classical literature is a phenomenon much more widespread than Beaton implies; and it is not only an attempt to legitimize the creation of a new genre, but a whole communicative code of reference used by late antique authors and based on the fully developed system of education, an education which was taken over wholesale by the Byzantines.[73] Literary allusion (be it direct quotation or indirect reference)[74] is not an antiquarian trait of the Byzantine *psyche*, but an educationally ingrained concept of conservationist cultural unity. Therefore, to interpret the intertextual references in Byzantine literature as an attempt to recapture the past and redefine an identity as inheritor of a Hellenistic age is anachronistic and oversimplified. Beaton asks himself why the Byzantine authors of the 12th century romances do not allude to 'the coming of Christianity, to the existence of Constantinople, or to almost a thousand years of Byzantine history' (54). How is it possible for a Byzantine author striving to imitate the ancient novel to refer to such things? Does Heliodoros refer to his own time? Of course not!

Moreover, Beaton does not understand the operative principle of *mimesis*, when he says that the openings of Prodromos' and Eugenianos' works 'refer us immediately to the opening of the *Aithiopika* (and through it to the Homeric periphrases involving the chariot of the sun) and so declare the nature of the text that we are embarking upon'

---

[73] Concerning certain aspects of Middle Byzantine education and its firm roots in Late Antiquity, see A.Markopoulos, 'Η οργάνωση του σχολείου. Παράδοση και εξέλιξη', in: *Η καθημερινή ζωή στο Βυζάντιο. Τομές και συνέχειες στην ελληνιστική και ρωμαϊκή παράδοση*. Πρακτικά του Α' διεθνούς συμποσίου 15-17 Σεπτεμβρίου 1988 (Athens 1989) 325-333 (with full bibliography).

[74] Carried away, it seems, by the supposedly abounding references and allusions to the older romances, Beaton goes so far as to toy with the absurd idea that the *characters* in the 12th century novels have read the Hellenistic works: on p. 52 he argues that 'if the hero is assumed to know Achilles Tatios' romance ... then he has good grounds for being alarmed ... ' One's mind boggles at the thought; but it is as good a case of 'Lady Macbeth's children' as any. See L.C.Knights, *How Many Children Had Lady Macbeth?* (Cambridge 1933). Presumably, this is also the reason why in detective fiction the butler is never afraid when the police arrives - the butler knows from his reading, as we all do, that it is never the butler who committed the murder, although the initial suspicion must concentrate on him, for the sake of suspense. He might as well be afraid, however, because παρὰ προσδοκίαν he may after all be the culprit.

(52). This is exactly what is not happening in the two Byzantine novels. The opening of the *Aithiopika*, which indicates the hour of the first action-tableau, has its own structure and cannot be considered as including any reference to Homer. The introduction of the Homeric motif (which is a quintessential temporal structural device in the two Byzantine works, as it is not in the *Aithiopika*) elevates the romances to an epic diction (wholly absent from Heliodoros) accentuated by the use of the iambic trimeter, and thus distances the Byzantines from their structural (and not necessarily conceptual) model.[75] In no way can we accept the idea that the Komnenian authors attempted 'to recapture, in the fictional world they create, the world of the past in which that literature took shape' (54). This statement imports a false notion of historical perspective, which as we have stated above, is not plausible for the Komnenian age. Nowhere is the 'past' of the romances expressly referred to as such. The authors make no attempt whatsoever to create a gap between theirs and the previous age imitated. The reason for this lies probably more in the fact that coherent imitation of older literary genres is perceived as an excellent possibility for artistic creation, than in an anxiety syndrome of an age in crisis.

The second thematic element concerns the motif 'Love as tyrant'. Beaton is blatantly contradicting himself, when he suggests innovations on one hand and development from Hellenistic literature on the other. The 12th century authors offer no innovations whatsoever on the question of Eros as a brutal tyrant, that is, Eros as a negative force (in this sense the quest for salvation through love becomes once again problematic). Even the idea of Eros as king/emperor is found in the ancient texts; but the gradual expansion of this particular feature (the imperial nature of the god) is something peculiarly Byzantine and does reflect a different approach to 'authority'. One must not forget that Christ is also a βασιλεύς, that the Byzantine emperor is often characterized by divine attributes and that Christ and emperor are the highest instances of their respective domains of power. Eros, therefore, as the highest authority in the romances is described by the attributes of authority best known to the Byzantines.[76]

'Love and death' is the subject of the third thematic element taken over by the

---

[75] See also Agapitos, *Narrative Structure* 233-235 and 238-239. Compare the 'Homeric' openings of *Rhodanthe* and *Drosilla* with the Heliodorean imitation in Bryennios i 16 (Gautier 113, 19-20) Ἡμέρας δ' ἤδη διαγελώσης καὶ τοῦ ἡλίου ὁρίζοντα ὑπερβαίνοντος.

[76] For the bureaucratic colouring of Eros' domain (the Ἐρωτοκρατεία) see H. Hunger, 'Die Herrschaft des Buchstabens. Das Verhältnis der Byzantiner zu Schrift- und Kanzleiwesen', Δελτίον τῆς Χριστιανικῆς Ἀρχαιολογικῆς Ἑταιρείας iv 12 (1984) 17-38. espec. 30ff (now reprinted in *Epidosis. Gesammelte Schriften zur byzantinischen Geistes- und Kulturgeschichte* [München 1989]). On the relation between Emperor and Christ as used in literature see P. A. Agapitos, 'Ἡ εἰκόνα τοῦ αὐτοκράτορα Βασιλείου Α' στὴν φιλομακεδονικὴ γραμματεία 867-959'. Ἑλληνικά 40 (1989) 285-322. especially 292-294.

Byzantines from the late antique novels. Beaton primarily discusses the various death scenes in the romances, and although he once again rejects the idea of 'mystery religions or actual ritual' (57), he nevertheless superimposes some kind of initiation pattern for the protagonists. Interestingly enough, the Byzantine authors do not include as many deaths, while no initiation patterns emerge and the quest for salvation must once again appear problematic. Moreover, Beaton never makes clear for the reader exactly what he means by 'love and death'. There are a number of recent theories from psychological to social points of view on this question which he does not touch upon at all to elucidate his suggestions (e.g. Bataille, Foucault, Vernant just to mention French theoreticians[77]). Furthermore, he shows lack of familiarity with the ancient material when he suggests that 'Evyenianos makes use of the love-death equation in its characteristically modern Greek guise, in a love-letter which links Eros with Charon' (57). This equation goes back at least to the erotic epigrams in Book 5 of the *Greek Anthology*, and it cannot have a characteristically modern Greek guise when it appears in a 12th century text.[78]

Fourth among the thematic elements is 'Chance and the passive hero'. Beaton argues that 'the inactivity of the main characters in the face of Chance and of a domineering god of love amounts in the ancient romances to the status of a theme, and as such is considerably extended in the romances of the twelfth century' (59). We would like to point out first of all that if this is so, then the quest for salvation is once again seriously devaluated as a central idea, since the characters are *a priori* chosen for each other; the god of Love or Chance determine their lives, irrespective of what they may say and do. One should add here that divine determination and the resulting role of man (paralleled by the unquestionably pagan notion of Τύχη) was discussed in Byzantine

---

[77] The list could easily be prolonged but we confine ourselves to a tradition referred to by Beaton himself.

[78] The reference to Margaret Alexiou's article on Charon ('Modern Greek folklore and its relation to the past: the evolution of Charos in Greek tradition', in: S.Vryonis (ed.): *Βυζαντινά και Μεταβυζαντινά 1* [Malibu 1978] 221-236) is misleading because she does not discuss Eros at all. Moreover, the development Charon-Charos = Thanatos goes back to Christian lyrical poetry of the 4th century (Gregorios Nazianzenos) and rhetoric (Ioannes Chrysostomos) and is fully established by the 11th century (Psellos' funerary poem on Maria Skleraina edd. Kurtz-Drexl [Milano 1936] and ed. Maria Dora Spadaro [Catania 1984]).

times throughout, not only in the 12th century.⁷⁹ It is not so easy to deduce a Christian virtue out of the characters' inactivity, and one should keep in mind that the complex notion of ἀπάθεια was in existence well before the rise of Christianity.⁸⁰ On the other hand it is during the Komnenian age that the powers of the individual and its active role in its own life are stressed by the historical works concerning Emperor Alexios I, namely the almost romance-like *Hyle historias* of Nikephoros Bryennios and the prose epic *Alexias* by Anna Komnene. It is questionable therefore to see in the inactivity of the romance characters a reflection of a Christian background or the creation of a bleak world as an attempt to evade any contemporary allusion. We would suggest that the 12th-century authors saw in their models the potential for effectful scenes of pathos, and this is a quintessential trait of rhetorical composition. The romances appear as a series of canvases,⁸¹ where various πάθη and ἤθη are acted out in strict observation of traditional rhetorical techniques; causality in any psychological sense is totally absent. Beaton rightly points out that Makrembolites calls his novel a δρᾶμα.⁸² This is nothing new; Photios had done the same for the ancient novel.⁸³ What has to be stressed here, is that δρᾶμα does not mean 'something done' for the Byzantines (so Beaton 219 n.19) in the

---

[79] See the comprehensive analysis of the determination of the hour of death with the concomitant question of divine will by P. Hildebrand Beck O.S.B. (H.-G. Beck), *Vorsehung und Vorherbestimmung in der theologischen Literatur der Byzantiner* [Orientalia Christiana Analecta 114] (Roma 1937); on *Tyche* see *id., Theodoros Metochites. Die Krise des byzantinischen Weltbildes im 14. Jahrhundert* (München 1952) 96ff. Beaton's statement that Manassis was the first to introduce the image of the wheel of Fortune is incorrect. In Plutarch's *Demetrios* 45,3 the author suggests that the hero's fortunes are continuously rotating; he exemplifies this with a quotation from a lost play by Sophocles fr.871 (Stefan Radt, *Tragicorum graecorum fragmenta* 4: *Sophocles* [Göttingen 1977]): ἀλλ' οὑμὸς ἀεὶ πότμος ἐν πυκνῷ θεοῦ / τροχῷ κυκλεῖται καὶ μεταλλάσσει φύσιν (with Radt's commentary on the passage).

[80] See the *Index* compiled by Max Adler in: J. von Arnim (ed.), *Stoicorum veterum fragmenta* iv (Leipzig 1924) s.v. ἀπάθεια.

[81] The pathetic monologue as lament, the beautiful banquet, the exquisite garden, the horrifying magical practices, the tender love-scene, the comic scene etc.

[82] *Hysm.* xi 23.3 (ed. Hercher, *Erotici scriptores graeci* [Lipsiae 1859] ii 286, 13-15) κλῆσις δ' ἔσται τῇ βίβλῳ τὸ καθ' Ὑσμίνην δρᾶμα καὶ τὸν Ὑσμινίαν ἐμέ. Add to this that some manuscripts include an actual *hypothesis* in iambic trimeters (Hilberg p. lxxxviii); the same is true about the *hypothesis* of Eugenianos' work (ed. Hercher, *op. cit.* ii 436).

[83] *Bibl.* 87.66a 27 (Henry ii 11), 94.73b 28-29 (Henry ii 34) etc. On the whole question of terminology, see Agapitos, *Narrative Structure* 43-44 and G. Giatromanolakis (ed.), Ἀχιλλέως Ἀλεξανδρέως Τατίου Λευκίππη καὶ Κλειτοφῶν (Athens 1990) 719-734.

sense of the Aristotelian τὰ δρώμενα; it means 'tragedy', 'plot', 'conspiracy'.[84] Consequently, when Makrembolites uses the term he implies the profusion of sorrowful and horrid events in the plot of the work (the logical misunderstanding of Aristotelian ἔλεος καὶ φόβος), as well as a 'theatrical' approach to the composition of the text. Theatrical, of course, cannot mean dramaturgical. It suggests that since tragedy was perceived as the instance forcing upon a 'passive' audience sorrowful events,[85] then a romance plot can take up this element and explore it. The canvases of set-pieces present in the Komnenian novels are nothing but a series of 'tragedy' scenes inflicted upon the characters of the work. With the happy end the novel itself ends and the characters leave the stage of their romance life untouched by the 'theatrical' (*qua* rhetorical) horrors. It is no coincidence that the Komnenian works abound in references to tragedy and use tragic vocabulary for the framing of numerous scenes of pathos.[86]

The strained attempt by Beaton to find developmental 'pointers' (61) to the *Digenis* in the romances lacks all foundation, since the elopement-motif is central to the ancient romances; it is not an abduction, because the heroine is fully informed and consents to the plans. Consequently, the *Digenis* remains a work *sui generis* with no actual interconnections to the 12th century texts.

Last in the list of thematic elements is the subject 'Art and nature: description'. Beaton presents the reader with yet another generalizing statement about the ancient romances being self-conscious literary experiments with the exception of Xenophon's *Ephesiaka* (62). It is not within our purpose to discuss the nature of the late antique texts, but we would like to point to the by now leit-motivic use of the word 'self-conscious' by Beaton. He never explains what he means, especially since he suggests that it is the work that is self-conscious, rather than its author, which - despite the

---

[84] For a superb use of the word in both the sense of 'tragic scene' and 'set up' see Bryennios ii 24 (Gautier 193, 3-12), where Roussel is presented by Alexios to the people of Amaseia as a 'new Oedipus': ἔωθεν δὲ πρὸς τὸ πλῆθος ἐξάγεται καὶ ὁρᾶται παρὰ πάντων ὡς δῆθεν τυφλός· τοῦτο τὸ δρᾶμα πάμπαν τὸν θόρυβον κατεσίγασεν. Later on, when Alexios discloses his trick to Theodoros Dokeianos, the latter τὸ δρᾶμα ἐπήνει καὶ τὴν σκηνὴν ἐθαύμαζε (Gautier 197, 7-8).

[85] This misconception of Greek Tragedy is found already in the Roman theatre and was later taken up by Renaissance and Baroque dramatists.

[86] See Agapitos, *Narrative Structure* 209.

propositions of post-structuralist semioticians[87] - is not the same thing. We are tempted to see here the use of a modernistic term camouflaging a trite aesthetic statement, namely that the particular work is 'good' (why should the *Ephesiaka* be less self-conscious than the *Aithiopika*?). Beaton proceeds to give a partial illustration of his point by referring to the system of allusions in the romances. This is, according to Beaton, an artifice of illusion: 'in order to foster the illusion that the reader actually sees the scene described on the page, the writer must appeal to the techniques of representation used in the visual arts. It is a technique the opposite of realism as it was understood in the nineteenth century: nature is revered only insofar as it conforms to the laws of art, and not the other way about' (63). What follows is a catalogue of descriptions and references by the author to a mythological prototype (x and y are like Aphrodite or Achilles). What we said earlier about the nature of textual quotations is true about what we could term cultural quotations. To describe a person (be it actual or fictional) by means of a mythological prototype gives the necessary cultural nexus to both author and reader in order to communicate, while at the same time the subject is elevated to a higher status. That this has nothing to do with realism is obvious, but it has also nothing to do with artifice and it does not make the work self-conscious. It only goes to show the importance and power of the 'authoritarian' cultural heritage, common to literati and public of a given age. And this is a phenomenon of a much earlier date than Beaton lets the reader believe, and, of course, of a much broader scope as well.[88] At the same time, the techniques of the *ekphrasis* fulfill a similar function. It must be remembered that descriptions of works of art (most of which had mythological subjects) were independent literary works (e.g. the *Eikones* of the two Philostratoi) separate from the specific descriptions in progymnasmatic collections. The incorporation of descriptions in the late antique novels (be it the plot-tableau of Heliodoros or the works of art in Tatios) is determined by the rhetorical referentiality needed between author and reader to establish a common ground,

---

[87] See, e.g. the rejection of authorial self-consciousness in Michael Riffaterre, *La production du texte* (Paris 1979), *id.*, *Fictional Truth* (Baltimore 1990), followed by younger critics like Alexandre Leupin, *Barbarolexis. Medieval Writing and Sexuality* (Cambridge, Mass. 1989). For a sensitive and sensible criticism of Riffaterre's method see P. de Man, 'Hypogram and Inscription: Michael Riffaterre's Poetics of Reading', Diacritics 11.4 (1981) 17-35 (repr. in *id.*, *The Resistance to Theory*, foreword by Wlad Godzich [Theory and History of Literature 33] [Minneapolis 1986] 27-53).

[88] All ancient Greek lyric poetry uses this very system of cultural (*qua* mythical or ritual) reference; see, e.g., Sappho's marriage poem (cf. D. L. Page, *Sappho and Alcaeus* [Oxford 1955] 70-74) with the grand mythological reference to Hektor and Andromache (fr. 44 L.-P.). So does Hellenistic and imperial literature (Plutarch's *Antonios* is an excellent example, where Antonios is juxtaposed to Dionysos).

as well as being part of the author's demonstration of his skill.⁸⁹ The Byzantines took over this system both in their 'pagan' education, as well as in their Christian beliefs (the Bible is just such a reference system).

We do not want to say that the Byzantines did not have a conscious approach to literary composition. But the presence of descriptions in the Komnenian romances is not enough to elevate them to the status of 'self-conscious literary experiments'. Beaton concentrates on four examples to demonstrate that art substitutes nature and that while nature vanishes, art remains. There are two references to nature in Prodromos and one in Makrembolites: Nature is a geometer who has formed Rhodanthe into perfection (*Rhod.* ii 249-50).⁹⁰ We fail to see where the author in this passage says anything about his own work. The next two passages are indeed most interesting: A cup is described that just broke (*Rhod.* iv 329-411). But does this imply that art endures? Is it not more simple to suggest that the power of *mimesis* endures? Similarly, the reference to the complex and strange form of four people (τετρακτύς) embracing each other (*Rhod.* ix 320ff) is a classic case of a rhetorical *paradoxon* explained by means of a simile to woven clothes or tapestries.⁹¹ Moreover, the 'wise geometer' producing this effect (*Rhod.* ix 336) is not nature nor the author's art, but 'the hand of joy' (ἡ τῆς χαρᾶς χείρ). What is interesting in this passage, as in the previous one, is the personal choice of Prodromos to use a geometer craftsman (be it nature or joy) who creates a beautiful image (be it a woman or a paradoxical figure).

The last example on art and nature comes from Makrembolites: 'the closing pages of the romance in which salvation that has been sought throughout the ancient and the

---

⁸⁹ On descriptions in the novels see Shadi Bartsch, *Decoding the Ancient Novel. The Reader and the Role of Description in Heliodorus and Achilles Tatius* (Princeton, N. J. 1989) although the author does not concentrate enough on the educational background and social function of rhetoric in Late Antiquity.

⁹⁰ The correct translation of the passage is 'for geometer Nature shaped her beautifully and orderly' (καλῶς γὰρ αὐτὴν καὶ κεκανονισμένως / ἐσχημάτισεν ἡ γεωμέτρις φύσις) and not 'for this was beautiful and according to rules shaped by the geometer Nature'. Unfortunately, this is not the only mistranslation in Beaton's quotations from the texts. One of the most remarkable howlers can be found on p. 55 where the passage from *Dros.* iii 17 Ἔρωτι δόξαν τῷ τυράννῳ is translated as a 'parody' of the liturgical formula 'glory be to Eros the tyrant' (this is even repeated on p. 153), whereas the meaning is of course 'decided by Eros the tyrant'. For other cases see nn. 58, 92, 99, 201 and 248.

⁹¹ Models for this kind of similes are found in the *Odyssey* (Penelope weaving the cloth to delay the suitors) and the *Argonautica* (Apoll. Rhod. i 721-768; see the commentary with further examples in F.Vian [ed.], *Apollonios de Rhodes. Argonautiques,* tome i [2e ed. Paris 1976] 83-86). Furthermore, it is doubtful if Prodromos ever thought of τετρακτύς in Pythagorean terms, since in Byzantine lexicographical usage it normally means 'unit of four' = τετράς. or refers to the four basic disciplines learned at school, the Western *quadrivium*.

twelfth century romances is equated with the permanence of "a golden statue hammered out of words" (*Hysm.* ix 22)' (65-66). The passage referred to, which figures also as a motto to Beaton's book, is the key to his conception of the romance as salvation through art, be it 'salvation sought literally by the hero and heroine in these stories, and vicariously, it may be supposed by their authors and first readers or audiences' (66). However, this is also the only passage in the Komnenian romances offering such a possibility of interpretation and Beaton expounds it in full (84). We would like to remark that while indeed the gods are not as trustworthy as the power of words in this passage, the author includes two concepts that make the salvation idea problematic, or at least tentative. In the first instance Makrembolites distinguishes clearly between 1) the protagonist's story which is to be 'depicted on a στήλη by means of Hermes' pen and ink and by a tongue breathing a rhetorical fire just like in <the case of> evergreen trees and diamonds' (ἀλλ' ὡς ἐν ἀμαράντοις ξύλοις καὶ λίθοις ἀδάμασιν Ἑρμοῦ γραφίδι καὶ μέλανι καὶ γλώττῃ πῦρ πνεούσῃ ῥητορικὸν τὰ καθ' ἡμᾶς στηλογραφηθήσεται),[92] and 2) the handing down of this story to later generations by means of an ὀψίγονός τις. This is a distinction between story (actual event) fixed by whatever means and the 'golden statue hammered out in words' by a later narrator (the work itself). Secondly, the author uses the phrase 'Hermes' pen and ink', by itself an interesting image, since Hermes is the god protecting both heralds (as Hysminias is in the romance) and of orators (since Hysminias is the first-person narrator). 'Hermes' pen and ink' is then a recherché periphrasis for the 'art of rhetoric', and it is indicative that the pen and ink is paralleled by the tongue of the orator. Finally, the word ἀνδριάς ('statue') has another function in Byzantine literature as well, since it immediately evokes in the Byzantine reader the specific image of paraenetic literature: 'the work is like a statue which is to be admired and imitated'.[93]

To sum up: the text is in reality elusive; narrator and author are different, the

---

[92] Beaton's translation both distorts the syntax and the meaning of the passage ('then, as though in unfading timbers and in adamantine precious stones, in Hermes' script and ink and in language breathing the fire of rhetoric let our experiences be inscribed'). But ἀμάραντα ξύλα are 'evergreen trees', not 'unfading timber', which obviously makes no sense, for the ὡς ἐν is the usual comparative conjunction + preposition for the *illustrans*. And γραφίς means 'pen' and not 'script'; furthermore, τὰ καθ' ἡμᾶς (sc. πράγματα) are not 'our experiences', but 'our story' which makes a big difference. Finally, γλῶττα here means literally the tongue, i.e. the mouth as the faculty of speech, not the language used. Makrembolites carefully applies very concrete and not abstract images.

[93] On the genre of βασιλικοὶ ἀνδριάντες see *Byzantinische Fürstenspiegel. Agapetos, Theophylakt von Ochrid, Thomas Magister.* Übersetzt und erläutert von W. Blum [Bibliothek der griechischen Literatur 147] (Stuttgart 1981) 1-58 and Hunger, *Profanliteratur* i 157-165.

rhetorical framework suggests imitation, canonization, fixation and not movement towards a salvation of the hero, much less of the author. The resulting picture is that Beaton's reasoning for the 'renaissance of a genre' (and the background he describes) appears problematic in its haphazard selection of conventional *topoi*, presented in a seemingly modern guise, but remaining ultimately conservative.[94]

---

[94] Beaton says almost nothing (50) about the much discussed attempt by Herbert Hunger to see what he calls 'Aktualisierungsversuche' in the literature of the Komnenian period ('Die byzantinische Literatur der Komnenenzeit. Versuch einer Neubewertung', Anzeiger der Österreichischen Akademie der Wissenschaften, philos.-hist. Klasse 105, 1968, reprinted in *Byzantinische Grundlagenforschung* [London 1973]), which does injustice to Hunger's work, even if one does not agree.

Chapter 6

The first 'modern Greek' literature

The first section of Chapter 6 discusses 'The Rise of Vernacular Literature', the character of the language and the 12th century works where the vernacular appears as a literary medium.

Some of the basic ideas in this chapter are rather unclear. Beaton claims that on one hand there is a remarkable continuity in the early 14th century with the 12th century, on the other he speaks of a development, and of the sudden emergence of the vernacular as the unchallenged medium for almost all literary fiction (for a moment forgetting what he said about the vernacular in the *Digenis*). Although he is rightly stressing the political turmoil at the time, this does not seem to affect his argument. One misses an emphasis on the point that compared to the masses of traditional writing in the Palaiologian era, the few vernacular works are no more than a drop in the ocean.

Beaton here (88-89) mentions the other vernacular texts from the period, the chronicles and the allegories (*Poulologos* etc.). Some of his statements call for comment. The *Chronicle of the Morea* is said to 'be dated to the first part of the fourteenth century' and to be 'one of the earliest vernacular poems that can be accurately dated in this period'. Beaton is probably here basing himself on M. Jeffreys' paper on the *Chronicle*,[95] in which Jacoby's dating of the MS *Haun. Fabr.* 57 to the 1380's was accepted, and the priority of the Greek version was argued. If the Greek text is prior to the French as has been forcefully set forth by Jeffreys, the date of the Copenhagen MS is not so important. Still, in view of the imprecise dating in most literature on the subject, we would like to

---

[95] 'The Chronicle of the Morea: priority of the Greek version', BZ 68 (1975) 304-350.

emphasize that the watermarks in the book definitely point to the decade 1360-1370.[96] And as for the earliest datable text, one would like to see the *Kallimachos* mentioned.[97]

Beaton then goes on to claim that the *Chronicle* 'is generally agreed to be the closest surviving witness to the spoken idiom at the time' (88). It is very difficult to know what he implies, for on the next page he emphatically rejects the notion that these texts are the 'spoken Greek of the time transferred to parchment' (somewhat maliciously one might object that no vernacular text was ever written on parchment); a few lines later (89) he quotes Beck for the opinion that the language of these texts was the spoken idiom of the capital (we might add that Beck never said such a thing, even though Beaton refers to *Volksliteratur* 9 and 'Leserkreis' 48). Finally, he settles for the totally unverified idea of a 'Kunstsprache',[98] and forgets about the *Chronicle* being the closest surviving witness to the spoken idiom of the time. One of the main characteristics of this language, according to Beaton, is the extravagant coining of compound words, a feature also to be found in the vernacular of the 12th century, though Prodromos is not mentioned here - probably because in this author the coining of comical compounds has more to do with imitation of Aristophanes than with Byzantine usage. No doubt the *ekphraseis* in the romances are heavily loaded with such compounds, and the examples quoted from the **N** version of the *Achilleid* (813 and 816-820) and from *Florios* (190-194) are fair

---

[96] See Schartau's catalogue of the Greek MSS in the Copenhagen Royal Library *Codices graeci Haunienses. Ein deskriptiver Katalog des griechischen Handschriftenbestandes der Königlichen Bibliothek Kopenhagen* von Bjarne Schartau (forthcoming). On the subject of the *Chronicle* it is perhaps worth while to point out that the Paris MS of the text, *Par. gr.* 2898, once made up a separate book and has not been written by the same scribe who wrote the preceding text, the *Theseid*, in the MS. In fact, the Paris MS of the *Chronicle* has been written by two other and different hands which obviously change between f. 218r and 218v. That the Paris MS once was two different codices can be seen from the separate numbering of the quires in the second part of the book on f. 126v β' and f. 134v γ'. Cf. also David Jacoby, 'Quelques considerations sur la version de la "Chronique de Morée"', Journal des Savants 1968, 159 n. 113 on the watermarks in the Paris MS and 155 n. 93 on the Copenhagen MS. See also below n. 177.

[97] We return to this below p. 55f.

[98] The theory of an artificial language as a result of a long epic tradition was fair enough in the case of Homer, and no one would question that today, even if we now think more in the way of Parry-Lord about the 'Kunstsprache' than in the way of the German philologists who coined the term (cf. Karl Meister, *Die homerische Kunstsprache* [Leipzig 1921]). But it is a wholly different thing to regard the vernacular in the romances as a 'Kunstsprache', as the 'proud' creation of the Byzantine poets.

enough (except for some mistranslations which do not affect the argument[99]), but to our mind Beaton's view is too general and too little fortified with quantitive arguments to be convincing. In fact, it would be a useful and obvious research project to investigate both these compound words (and establish a reliable statistic material) in the vernacular texts and the whole problem of the 'Kunstsprache'. So little has been done in linguistic analysis of these texts that an off-hand judgment such as Beaton's, based, it seems, mostly on a few pages in Browning's *Medieval and Modern Greek,* [100] really is unacceptable.

Beaton then addresses himself to the question of why the vernacular was used sporadically in the 12th century (91). Beaton claims that the *Ptochoprodromika* contain more or less explicit comments on their author's choice of linguistic medium, which is not so easy to see in all the poems, and Beaton's arguments do not lend support to this. We cannot see, e.g., in the case of the fourth poem that Prodromos says, or implies anything about his choice of linguistic level, nor that a contrast between the learning of the narrator and the speech of the humble tradesman is invited (92). There is, however, an absolutely clear case in the ptochoprodromic *corpus* where the author signals the change of linguistic register (albeit a short one), but Beaton makes no use of it. In the so-called Maiuri-poem[101] the poet ends his plea to the emperor for more financial support with a switch in diction as follows (vv. 64-66):

τρεῖς χρόνους, μὰ τὸ κράτος σου καὶ μὰ τὴν κεφαλήν σου,

οὐκ οἶδα ἐκ τὸ βεστιάριν σου χαλκοῦν, ὁλοκοτίνιν,

καί, ἂν τὸ εἴπω κορακιστικόν, τζιρίζουσι τὰ βράκη.

The highly proverbial phrase τζιρίζουσι τὰ βράκη (an obvious 'drop' in register from the more or less conventional diction of the previous verses) is introduced with the marker κορακιστικόν, a word that has negative connotations, meaning 'gibberish', 'parler des enfants'. It is attested in Ioannes Chrysostomos, as well as Modern Greek usage.[102] What the word suggests is that this particular linguistic register is perceived as 'funny', deviating from the norm.

Discussion of the *Spaneas* is not wholly satisfactory either. The non-specialist

---

[99] In the *Ach.* **N** 818 Beaton translates the formulaic γέννημα τῶν χαρίτων as 'giving birth to graces' whereas it means 'child of the graces'. In line 819 ὑπεραναστα λμένη does not mean 'ultra-modest' but rather 'with glorious outward appearance'. In *Flor.* 191 he has gone awry of the word μαυροπλουμιστομάταν which compound he analysed wrongly as meaning 'dark-decorated-mouthed', instead of 'with dark-decorated eyes' or even 'decorated with dark eyes'.

[100] Robert Browning, *Medieval and Modern Greek* [2nd ed.] (Cambridge 1983) 84-85.

[101] See above n. 22.

[102] See Th. Ph. Papadopoulos, 'Κορακιστικά', Μεγάλη Ἑλληνικὴ Ἐγκυκλοπαίδεια 14 (1931) 867-868 and Kriaras, *Λεξικό* s.v.

will come away with the impression that G. Spadaro and G. Danezis agree about the character of this text, while it is not tenable to say that the *Spaneas* is a linguistic transposition of an earlier Byzantine handbook of ancient moral precepts (92).[103] It is also difficult to reconcile the two statements (*ibid.*) that *Spaneas* was widely read (at least to judge from the number of MSS), but played only a minor role in the development of the vernacular as a literary medium, especially since it is also claimed that it had some impact on the translated romances and on Falieros. The idea of Fyrigos quoted apparently with approval by Beaton (92-93) that the title *Spaneas* was given to the work from the advice in *Florios* given by the king of Spain (Σπανία) is ludicrous.[104]

To sum up, no one would query the conclusion that the evidence points to the vernacular being imposed from above, in so far as the literature belongs to the court milieu. Whatever 'a breakthrough of popular culture' might mean at the time, it is clear that conditions for literary production have not changed with the introduction of vernacular elements. To some extent, a different situation obtains in the 14th century; the problem is how to describe the difference. Beaton refers (93) to two papers by Beck[105] in summarizing 'that experiments in vernacular literature in the fourteenth century are initially, at least, a continuation of those in the twelfth. According to this view, the earlier texts of our period are the work of educated writers, self-consciously exploiting the possibilities of a new medium, while by the fifteenth century a new, genuinely popular literary stratum has begun to emerge'. To judge from what Beck actually said in these two papers, it is far from certain that he would recognize his own position in Beaton's summary. Apart from that, it is clear from Beck's analyses that he starts from the conviction that the earliest romance is the *Kallimachos*, and that it was written by Andronikos Palaiologos,[106] and from this perspective he sees the development from the 12th to the 14th and 15th centuries. As it turns out, Beaton's view is considerably different, because he puts as the earliest 'romance' a text that in Beck's view is much later and belongs to a different culture, namely the *Achilleid*.[107]

However, Beaton's views become wholly speculative at the end of this section when

---

[103] See Georg Danezis, *Spaneas: Vorlage, Quellen, Versionen* [Miscellanea Byzantina Monacensia 31] (München 1987). See also the discussion between Spadaro and Danezis implicit in H. Eideneier (ed.), *Neograeca Medii Aevi* (Köln 1987) 89ff.

[104] A.Fyrigos, 'Σπανίας Σπανέας. Proposta per una interpretazione del termine e ipotesi sulla datazione dell' omonimo poema', Bolletino della Badia Greca di Grottaferrata n.s. 39 (1985) 39-56.

[105] No particular passages from 'Leserkreis' and *Die griechische volkstümliche Literatur* are quoted.

[106] See below p. 55f for our position on this question.

[107] See Beck, 'Leserkreis' 59, and more outspoken, *Volkstümliche Literatur* 131.

he discusses the revival after the 13th century (which may not have been so unproductive as seems to be implied). He believes (93-94) that a catalyst was needed to have literary people recognize what lay latent in the 'experiments' of the 12th century, and that this catalyst was the example of Western vernacular literature. For this, of course, there is absolutely no evidence at all, but as we shall see below, Beaton is willing to go most of the way with the scholars who have insisted in seeing Western influence where the inspiration could more reasonably be found in Byzantium itself.

The section on the political verse (95-97) is not particularly helpful and contains a number of strange statements, including a warning that the political verse had nothing to do with politics! Something has gone wrong at the opening of the section: for *variable* caesura, read *invariable*. The subject is complex and there is no agreement on the question of origin of the verse, whether popular or learned.[108] Beaton, however, will not only have the best of two worlds; he settles for a both-and, strengthened by a somewhat woolly judgment by Linos Politis; he also suggests that just like in his view the *Digenis* is a convergence of two traditions, the metre also is 'doubly born'. We cannot see how this can explain anything, nor can Beaton's idea that the widespread use of the 12-syllable verse in twelfth century literature, against the odium pertaining to 15-syllable verse, may be explained with the argument that the 12-syllable verse *looked* like an iambic trimeter (this is the argument of a silent modern reader) in contrast to the political verse which had no such precedent. Apart from the fact that nobody could be deceived by the 12-syllable verse as soon as it was read aloud, it should be mentioned that if a precedent along such lines had any meaning for the Byzantines, they had one in the trochaic tetrameter, as Eustathios, Planudes and an anonymous scholiast on Aeschylus, *Persae* 155 saw.[109] As if the authors of the romances might have cared for the origin of the verse they used, there is no trace, as far as we are aware, of any discomfiture (Beaton 97) felt by them in using this metre, and we are not helped very much, even if it could be proved that they must have felt so.

---

[108] For a useful critical review of literature on the question see Margaret Alexiou and David Holton, 'The origins and development of "politikos stichos"', Μαντατοφόρος 9 (1976) 22-34.

[109] The scholiast in the MS *Laur. plut.* 86,3 comments on the trochaic tetrameters spoken by the chorus 155-158: ση(μείωσαι) ὡς λέγουσί τινες ὡς ἐκ τούτων τῶν πολιτικῶν στίχων ἐπεκράτησεν ἡ συνήθεια τοῦ διὰ πολιτικῶν στίχων ποιεῖν τὰ τῶν βασιλέων προσφωνήματα. See on this scholium and its evidence for the political verse in Byzantium Michael J. Jeffreys & Ole L. Smith, 'Political Verse for Queen Atossa', ClMed 42 (1991) 303-306.

Chapter 7

The original romances: the texts and the stories

Beaton divides his treatment of the romances in two parts, referring to Gerard Genette's distinction between narrative content and narrative discourse (98) which is of no practical relevance here, since his discussion in this chapter is a fairly traditional and straightforward presentation of the problems of authorship, date and manuscript tradition. Once again, Beaton uses terminology of modern literary theory to camouflage a very conventional analysis. Moreover, he misrepresents Genette's views, dwindling them down to some superficial construct, which they are decidedly not.[110] In fact, it is highly probable that Beaton's understanding of Genette comes not from a closer reading of the French critic's substantial *oeuvre*,[111] but from the secondary source Beaton happened to use at the time.[112]

He points out (98) that there is no generic term for these texts, nevertheless he claims that there is 'an impressive degree of cohesion among the romances ... which suggests an implicit awareness of a common genre', a statement which he then goes on to contradict by adding that 'it may be that the writers of our period had a more open-ended concept of the genre in which they were working than is assumed here'. Unfortunately, as the reader will have noticed by now, this is a widespread tendency in Beaton's dealing with his subject: he gives two (or more) mutually exclusive judgments which makes it difficult for the reader to see what his own view really is. As we have also pointed out

---

[110] There is a long tradition in the distinction between the material from which a story is made and the way in which this material is presented in the work of art; this tradition goes back to the Russian formalists (*fable - sujet*) and was taken up by French structuralists (*récit - narration*), Anglo-American critics (*story - plot*) and German semioticians (*Inhaltsform - Ausdrucksform*). See the introductory presentation by W. Haubrichs, 'Einleitung: Für ein Zwei-Phasen-Modell der Erzählanalyse. Ausdrucksform und Inhaltsform in mittelalterlichen und modernen Bearbeitungen der Gregoriuslegende', in: W. Haubrichs (ed.): *Erzählforschung 1. Theorien, Modelle und Methoden der Narrativik* [Zeitschrift für Literaturwissenschaft und Linguistik. Beiheft 4] (Göttingen 1976) 7-28.

[111] Among others the three volumes of *Figures* (Paris 1968-1972); furthermore *Mimologiques. Voyage en Cratylie* (Paris 1976), *Seuils* (Paris 1987) and, of course, *Nouveau discours du récit* (Paris 1983). One can profit from Genette's most recent publication *Fiction et diction* (Paris 1991), a collection of four essays on questions of narratology, rhetorics and the aesthetics of fiction.

[112] S. Chatman, *Story and Discourse. Narrative Structure in Fiction and Film* (Ithaca & London 1978).

above, we strongly disagree with this view of a cohesion among these texts and with Beaton's attempt to fit them into his Procrustean schemata.

To return to the idea of a generic term: most of the romances do have titles which include the words διήγησις or ἀφήγησις.[113] This does not imply generic cohesion, it is only an indication about the narrative material offered by the author to the reader.

No one would object to the view that the Palaiologian romances can be divided into two groups (98): the original compositions and the translations or adaptations of Western models. But perhaps Beaton should have pointed out that this 'natural' division does not mean that there never was or could be doubt as to which group a given text belongs, since it is a moot question to decide whether a text is an adaptation or a translation, even in how far it is an 'original'.[114]

In way of general introduction he states that the five original romances are usually dated to the 14th and 15th centuries, that they are all of them anonymous, and most of the extant witnesses date from after the fall of Constantinople. Literal accuracy cannot be expected of the scribes which is clear from the manuscript tradition. We will return to all these basic problems but it should be pointed out that they are so important that it simply will not do to state this as Beaton does without a warning to the non-specialist that there are more than one view about all of these problems. Moreover, the lack of consensus - a lack, one might add, to which Beaton himself points in his preface (see above, p. 9f) in order to excuse his detailed discussions of things long agreed upon by Western medievalists - should be held in mind when reading the individual entries on the five texts.

The only problem discussed at all here is the problem of the fidelity of the manuscripts, for the simple reason that the misconceptions in the following detailed exposition of the manuscripts have to be given some basis. Consequently, Beaton argues (99) that we must not expect the accuracy known from scribes working with the learned texts. This is of course nothing but a *petitio principii* and rests on no evidence. The scribes copying the vernacular texts were professional people applying the same

---

[113] See the proems to *Kall.* (διήγημα), *Belth.* (διήγησις), and *Liv.* (ἀφήγησις), and cf. Agapitos, *Narrative Structure* 45.

[114] The *Imberios* is hardly a conventional translation at all; there is also the problem that the *Florios* (which Beaton calls a fairly close translation) may be deceptively similar to the Western model - at least in editions based on the principle that this text *is* a translation. The *Imberios* is more like a loose adaptation, although existing editions probably give a false impression of agreement between the MSS. The *Theseid* and the *War of Troy*, on the other hand, are closer to being real translations in the modern sense. Cf. below p. 69f.

discipline to their work with vernacular texts as they did with learned literature.[115] The vast differences between the vernacular manuscripts can and should be explained in a different way. Besides, the few cases we have of surviving manuscripts copied from sources still extant show that within the usual limits scribes were copying faithfully what they had before them, for example the fragment Σ of *Livistros*[116] or the copies made from printed editions as, for example, *Vat. gr.* 1139 from a printed edition of a late text like the Ἀπόκοπος,[117] and the *Mutinensis* of *Belisarios*.[118] It should perhaps be emphasized here that when scholars offer the argument that a stemma of, e.g., *Spaneas* is impossible to construct because of the havoc wrought by the disrespectful scribes, they seem to forget that it is equally impossible to put up a stemma of say, e.g., Aeschylus - for what amounts to the same reasons.

No doubt we would be much better able to judge the whole question of the manuscript tradition if we had more MSS of the same text - as is the case in French, Italian and Spanish vernacular literature. But with only one manuscript of the *Kallimachos*, the *Belthandros*, the *Byzantine Iliad* and with few and widely divergent MSS of the *Livistros* and the *Achilleid,* we are in a situation radically different from that of the editor and textual critic of Western texts.

The case for a different approach to the question of copies, scribes and copyists in vernacular literature has been put much more forcefully by Elizabeth and Michael Jeffreys. They argue that the scribes of the vernacular texts would not even have understood what was meant by an accurate copy, by 'word-by-word and letter-by-letter reproduction'. The rule, according to the Jeffreys, is variation, and the identical copy 'an exception, or perhaps a lucky accident'. These scribes are, in their view, different from those who copied our classical texts.[119]

Against these arguments we would emphasize that the scribes who copied the vernacular texts were brought up in the same scriptoria as the scribes who copied the

---

[115] E. & M. Jeffreys, *Okeanos* 317 have some remarks on the 'different tactics' in the behaviour of the scribes depending on whether they copied 'formal language' or vernacular texts. The formal language, unfortunately, did not discourage personal intervention by the scribes, but their intervention can usually be explained in a much different way, namely as an attempt to make as correct a text as possible.

[116] See on this Agapitos, *Narrative Structure* 28.

[117] Cf. St. Alexiou's edition, Κρητικά χρονικά 17 (1963) 184ff.

[118] Cf. W. F. Bakker and A. F. van Gemert, Ἱστορία τοῦ Βελισαρίου. Κριτικὴ ἔκδοση τῶν τεσσάρων διασκευῶν μὲ εἰσαγωγή, σχόλια καὶ γλωσσάριο [Βυζαντινὴ καὶ νεοελληνικὴ βιβλιοθήκη 6] (Athens 1988) 53-54.

[119] *Okeanos* 313. At the end of their argument here on p. 314, the Jeffreys suddenly distinguish between learned and vernacular texts instead of between scribes.

classical texts. We have absolutely no evidence that there were two different schools at all, and from the style and character of the writing in e.g. *Par. gr.* 2898, *Esc.* Ψ. iv. 22, Vienna *theol. gr.* 244 or Naples iii. B. 27 there is nothing to show that these scribes were not professional people.[120] This also means that they received the same training by copying religious (perhaps also learned secular) texts. Furthermore, the absence of an orthography for the vernacular language is another factor that has to be taken into consideration when judging the performance of the scribes. There is no reason why they should not have known what a copy meant, and thus we have to explain the differences between the MSS in another way. The true explanation, we submit, is that within the usual limits the scribes copied conscientiously what was before them. It is the texts we have to explain, not the behaviour of the scribes. That we have e.g. two MSS of the *Florios* that can only by sorcery be considered copies of the same original shows that we have to do with versions, rather than with copies.

Beaton regards the *Achilleid* as the earliest romance (99), as a bridge between the heroic epic and the love romance. This is not his main argument, which rather seems to be the assumedly close connection with the *Digenis*. Without any discussion he takes it for granted that the *Digenis* was the model for the author of the *Achilleid*; he even goes so far as to say that the *Digenis* is the only vernacular text that can be thought of with absolute certainty to have been known to the author.[121] From a purely methodological point of view this is unacceptable. We can never speak of certainty unless we have to do with outright quotation or reference. There are no compelling proofs of that sort here; there are thematic similarities but we have no means of telling whether these could appear in both texts only because one borrowed from the other. In many ways the *Achilleid* is a wholly different text, and it would be well if scholars would try to read the *Achilleid* as if it was a text in its own right and not just a poor substitute for the older and more recognized work. Beaton is equally certain of the relation to Makrembolites. The painted Eros in the Achilleid is derived from *Hysmine and Hysminias*. That Achilles has the painting of Eros made in order to invoke the god, seems not to have made any impression on the source

---

[120] For published specimina of the Escorial and Vienna MSS see the plates in Tsavari's edition of the *Poulologos* (cf.above n.4 for full details) and for the Naples MS the plates in H. Schreiner, 'Die einleitenden Überschriften zu den von der gleichen Hand übelieferten Texten in Cod. Neap. Gr. III. AA. 9 und Cod. Neap. Gr. III. B. 27', Byzantinische Forschungen 11 (1966) 290-320.

[121] Beaton is not the first to do so, of course. K. Mitsakis in his dissertation Προβλήματα σχετικὰ μὲ τὸ κείμενο, τὶς πηγὲς καὶ τὴ χρονολόγηση τῆς Ἀχιλληίδος (Thessaloniki 1961) and R. Keydell, 'Achilleis. Zur Problematik und Geschichte eines griechischen Romans', Byzantinische Forschungen 6 (1979) 83-99 are prime examples of this tendency.

hunters.[122]

This early date for the *Achilleid* Beaton attempts to strengthen by accepting in a more cautious way Spadaro's and Bakker-Van Gemert's theories of the *Achilleid* having been the inspiration or source for wholescale borrowing in the *Imberios* and the *Belisarios*. We do not accept this reasoning, and will deal with these questions later.

Among the three versions of the *Achilleid*, Beaton regards the Naples text[123] as the best: 'we can be fairly confident that the **N** version gives us the substance if not the wording of the original poem' (100). We are not told why we can be that confident; on Beaton's own view what has happened at the end of the poem should make us feel uncomfortable, for some rash interpolator has been busy here (at least according to the *communis opinio* accepted by Beaton), so why not elsewhere? The proem may also be ascribed to a later reworking, so that if you insist on looking for originals, which we find to be a waste of time, there is more to be said for the London version (**L**) in the MS British Museum *Add.* 8241, once you have removed the prose and restored the verse -

---

[122] The votive offering of a στήλη for the moon in *Livistros* (**S** 634-635, 2891-2898) might be comparable to the scene in the *Achilleid*.

[123] The **N** text in the Naples MS iii. B. 27 has been edited by D.C.Hesseling, *L'Achilleide byzantine* publiée avec une introduction, des observations et un index [Verhandelingen der Koninklijke Akademie van Wetenschapen te Amsterdam, Afdeeling Letterkunde N. R. xix. 3] (Amsterdam 1919). Renata Lavagnini (Rivista di studi bizantini e neoellenici 6-7 [1969-70] 165) is much too courteous in calling this edition 'una buona edizione critica' and her corrections to Hesseling (which by no means are complete) *ibid.* 176-179 show why one cannot trust his text. Even in 1919 Byzantinists could do better than this. For descriptions of **N** see D. Michailidis, '*Palamedes rediens*. La fortuna di Palamede nel medioevo ellenico', Rivista di studi bizantini e neoellenici 8-9 (1971-1972) 271ff.; H.Schreiner, Byzantinische Forschungen 1 (1966) 290f (information from the Biblioteca Nazionale, Napoli); A.van Gemert, *Μαρίνου Φαλιέρου Ἐρωτικὰ ὄνειρα. Κριτικὴ ἔκδοση μὲ εἰσαγωγή, σχόλια καὶ λεξιλόγιο* [Βυζαντινὴ καὶ νεοελληνικὴ βιβλιοθήκη 4] (Thessaloniki 1980) 50. The MS can be dated by watermarks in the older part ff. 13-99, which according to van Gemert are *similar* to Briquet 5959 (1460-1475). A new analysis of the watermarks would be very welcome, and it is certainly much too optimistic to say, as Beaton does in his n. 7 (223-224), that van Gemert has satisfactorily redated the folios containing these texts, on the evidence of the watermark. It must be said here that Schreiner in his paper made the strange mistake to disbelieve his own eyes and accept the claim by his informant in the Naples library that the hand in the older part of **N** (ff.13-99) was identical to the hand found in the other famous vernacular Naples MS iii. Aa. 9. From the plates (Tafeln xxvi-xxxi) accompanying Schreiner's paper anyone can see that the hands are considerably different. Of course, this makes havoc of most of what Schreiner says in his paper. For this negative view of Schreiner's findings see also G. Kehagioglou, *Κριτικὴ ἔκδοση τῆς ἱστορίας Πτωχολέοντος* [Αριστοτέλειο Πανεπιστήμιο Θεσσαλονίκης. Επιστημονικὴ επετηρίδα Φιλοσοφικῆς σχολῆς. Παράρτημα 22] (Thessaloniki 1978) 248 n. 47. Kehagioglou's dating of the manuscript **N** *op. cit.* 13 is unfortunately based on the false supposition that **N** is not a composite manuscript. The Falieros part of **N** is much later, cf. below p. 110. On the two vernacular MSS Napoli III. B. 27 and III. Aa. 9 see now also G. Spadaro, 'Testi medievali greci in demotico tramandati in codici napolitani', Ιταλοελληνικά 1 (1988) 49-74.

which would be necessary, according to modern opinion, in order to restore the text.[124] Beaton does not mention the problems of the London version and seems not to know Benedikt Haag's edition and commentary.[125] The Oxford version in the MS Oxford, Bodleian Library *Auct.* T. 5. 24 (**O**) is written off as little more than a *précis*. The arguments for this view have not been discussed. The presentation of the texts is superficial and never comes to grips with the problems of the relation between the three versions and their individual difficulties.[126]

The moot point of the relation between the end of the **N** *Achilleid* and the *Byzantine Iliad* is still open for debate. Beaton seems to agree with those who hold that the *Achilleid* has been interpolated from Manasses' *Chronicle* and the *Iliad*. He takes Smith and Nørgaard[127] to task for having proposed a lost common source for both *Achilleid* and *Iliad* (not very helpfully, he says)[128] but has obviously no qualms about proposing such lost models for the *Kallimachos*.[129]

The discussion of the *Kallimachos* romance (101-102) is not much better. Beaton accepts without the slightest doubt that the author of the anonymous romance is Andronikos Palaiologos, the nephew of Michael VIII. We must admit, however, that Beaton is not the only scholar to do so, and perhaps it is high time to emphasize that the romance

---

[124] Beck, 'Leserkreis' 59 calls **L** the more important MS of the *Achilleid*. On the question of **L** it should be emphasized that we do not agree with Chatzigiakoumis 244f that **L** represents a linguistic simplification of the **N** version.

[125] *Die Londoner Version der byzantinischen Achilleis* (Diss. München 1919). Haag's edition has been justly criticized, see for instance the damning verdict of Xanthoudides in Byz.-Neugr. Jarhb. 2 (1921) 203-205. For all the faults of his edition, Haag at least was aware of the peculiar nature of the **L** text with its prose-like and hypermetric lines. Haag's heavy-handed attempt to deal with these problems by wholesale emendation did not convince anybody, and his work has met with a not wholly justified neglect.

[126] The Oxford version has been discussed by Ole L. Smith cf. n. 61. For the Oxford MS we are still unable to reach a more certified date than the 16th century. The hands are extremely difficult to date, and the whole problem of the connection between the Oxford vernacular MSS raised by Sp. Lambros in *Collection des Romans Grecs en langue vulgaire et en vers* (Paris 1880) cxif. has not been dealt with as far as we are aware. For the text of the Oxford version see *The Byzantine Achilleid: The Oxford Version* edited by Ole L. Smith [Opuscula graecolatina edenda curavit Ivan Boserup Vol. 32] (Copenhagen 1990).

[127] In their edition of the text, L. Nørgaard & Ole L. Smith, *A Byzantine Iliad. The Text of Par. Suppl. Gr. 926*. Edited with Critical Apparatus, Introduction and Indexes [Opuscula graecolatina edenda curavit Ivan Boserup vol. 5] (Copenhagen 1975).

[128] It is interesting to see that one of the few scholars to have made an in-depth study of the *Byzantine Iliad*, Renata Lavagnini, also reaches the conclusion that we have to posit a lost common source for the two texts, cf. *I Fatti di Troia. L'Iliade bizantina del cod. Paris. suppl. gr. 936*. Introduzione, traduzione e note di Renata Lavagnini [Quaderni dell' Istituto di filologia greca della Universitá di Palermo 20] (Palermo 1988).

[129] We will return below p. 60 to the question of the Trojan end of the *Achilleid* and the relation to the *Byzantine Iliad*.

by Andronikos described in Manuel Philes' poem[130] does bear some resemblance to the *Kallimachos*, but it is impossible to identify the two (see below p. 106). What Philes' testimony bears out, however, is that such texts were produced at the imperial court around this time, and that is an important pointer for the date and social accept of these texts.[131] Beaton in his usual fashion does not commit himself on the problem of *Kallimachos*' chronological priority. What must be emphasized is that Philes' poem cannot be used to date the romance. Ultimately Beaton misrepresents the problem (in his note 12) which is not the high social standing of the presumed author but the differences between the *Kallimachos* text and the romance described by Philes.

Thus we are left, in our opinion, with the chronological problem open, and with an anonymous text like all the other, which may be the earliest, although we would argue that there is a case for *Livistros* to have preceded the other known romances.[132]

Since the Byzantines were incapable of writing anything without models in their minds and books on their tables, it is a problem in modern scholarship that there seem to be no obvious sources or models for the *Kallimachos*. Beaton states with some reason that the author knew the 12th century romances; there is on the other hand no evidence to suggest that he knew the *Digenis*, nor the *Achilleid* - if, as Beaton points out, that romance was already in existence. We agree that the (anonymous) author deserves a more important place in the history of Byzantine and Modern Greek literature, though not just because he happened to be the first - if that really is the case - but because of the literary qualities of the text.[133]

The text is transmitted, as is well known, in one MS only, Leiden *Scalig*. 55, 'believed to date from about 1520', says Beaton (102) referring to Chatzigiakoumis 36. This date was established by Pichard on the basis of the watermarks, and there is probably no reason to doubt it.[134] Here, as elsewhere, we have no means of determining the relation to the original. Beaton points out that in favour of its being a relatively close

---

[130] For an analysis of the poem see *Le Roman de Callimaque et de Chrysorrhoé*. Texte établi et traduit par Michel Pichard (Paris 1956) xvi-xxxi.

[131] Cf. Agapitos, *Narrative Structure* 16 n.16 with further references.

[132] See below p. 83. The whole question of the priority of the *Livistros* will be dealt with by P.A. Agapitos in the forthcoming acts of the *Neograeca Medii Aevi ii* conference.

[133] On this see P.A.Agapitos, ClMed 41(1990) 255ff where the highly sophisticated narrative is exemplified.

[134] Pichard, *op. cit.* (above n. 130) xxxiii. If, of course, and it is a big 'if', the watermark in the MS is exactly identical with Briquet 491. Pichard xxxiii n. 3 says that information about the watermark was given to him by the Leiden library, and he does not give any qualification to the identification. This mark belongs to a very common and widespread type ('ancre dans un cercle, surmonté d'une étoile') with several variations, so there might be a case for another look.

copy is the style and language of the text of the *Scaligeranus*. However, since Beaton ascribes to the dogma that scribes, especially in this period, tended to simplify the texts they copied, he adds that it would be 'naive to suppose that we possess the text exactly as written ... in the early fourteenth century' (102). The rubrics, he believes, are probably the work of a copyist. Again we emphasize that this opinion of the scribes is nothing more than a *fable convenue* and rests on no evidence - rather the opposite. The length to which scholars go who believe in the infidelity of the scribes is nowhere to be seen more clearly than here: Beaton thinks the *Scaligeranus* is a close copy, but such copies cannot exist if we are to believe what he says about the behaviour of the scribes. The underlying reasons for Beaton's high opinion of the MS is of course the literary quality of the text of the romance.

For some reason, Beaton comments here in the case of the *Kallimachos* on the rubrics which is a general feature in all the romances except for the *Belthandros*. This problem has never received the attention it deserves, and we do not regard the common opinion of the rubrics as the work of later copyists as justified in any way. We will return to it (below p. 68) and try to present a different point of view.

On the *Belthandros* Beaton is very brief (102). He seems to agree with others to reject Sigalas' and Schreiner's radical theories of the wholesale rewriting of the text,[135] and says that these ideas can now safely be put aside.[136] However, Chatzigiakoumis in the pages referred to does not say so but argues that the text should be edited as we have it in the MS (*Par. gr.* 2909) since there is nothing else we can do from a methodological point of view; he does not reject the theory that the text has been reworked in the sense that it may have been shortened and/or amplified, and superficially, at least, given a more 'modern' linguistic form. We cannot hope, in his opinion, to 'restore' the original text.[137] There is a further wrong reference to Chatzigiakoumis 213-215 who is adduced to support the idea that some of the elements of more popular speech and of oral folk song now in the text may not have been present in the original but may have come from the more popular texts in the MS. Chatzigiakoumis does not say so, and we are at a loss to see

---

[135] A.Sigalas, *Mélanges Merlier* ii (Athens 1956) 355-377; H.Schreiner, 'Zerrissene Zusammenhänge und Fremdkörper im Belthandros-Text', BZ 52 (1959) 257-264.

[136] With reference to Chatzigiakoumis 241-243; Beck, *Geschichte* 120-121; Kriaras, Ἱπποτικά μυθιστορήματα 89-96. Cf. now on the *Belthandros* also Lars Nørgaard, 'Byzantine Romance - Some Remarks on the Coherence of Motives', ClMed 40 (1989) 271-294. We would like to add here that we are out of sympathy with Lynda Garland's recent presentation of the case for *Belthandros* being close in atmosphere and conventions to the Western romances (BZ 82 [1989] 87ff).

[137] Cf. p. 242 ἡ ἀναγωγὴ στὸ πρωτότυπο παραμένει ἀνέφικτη.

how he came in here.[138] What he stresses, is the need for a scholarly edition of the text, a problem not mentioned by Beaton. It is far from certain that the text of the *Belthandros* has been 'creatively rewritten' in the way suggested by Beaton with partial linguistic simplification.[139] Rather one might tentatively propose that the text has been shortened, although without loss of the original plot-elements or a disorder in the narrative sequence. This can be seen, for example, from the way in which the speech frame functions in the romance. There are passages where the speech-frame formulas appear but no speech is included, while in sections where all the constituent parts of the discourse are present the text behaves in the conventional way.[140]

Perhaps it is fitting at this point to take up the editorial problem which Beaton until now has overlooked completely, but has to recognize in the case of the next romance, the *Livistros*. From his account so far one gets the impression that we have the editions we need in order to deal with more interesting questions such as literary criticism and comparative studies. The *Belthandros* is precisely a case in point, but the sorry state of editions of the *Achilleid* versions and the *Kallimachos*[141] is no less evident for anyone who looks into the manuscripts, or even takes the trouble to have a look into the - mostly ornamental - critical apparatuses. From our experience with the MSS of *Kallimachos*, *Belthandros*, *Livistros* and the *Achilleid* we feel confident in characterizing available editions as wholly insufficient and misleading. None of them - as has for some been argued forcibly by Chatzigiakoumis - meet even elementary needs of the reader nor requirements of scholars, be they linguists or literary critics. We are very far from having the tools we need for literary studies of Byzantine vernacular literature. This is not to say that such studies are now premature or lack foundation; it is possible to carry out research in vernacular literature, provided that one is aware of the problems and constantly recurs to the MSS themselves. We doubt, however, that Beaton ever worked on any of these manuscripts. Literary studies solely on the basis of most existing editions will lead nowhere except to false interpretations. This is exactly where one of our

---

[138] He mentions, however, that some elements from folk-song found in the *Florios* may be paralleled in *Belthandros* (p. 231 with n. 14).

[139] It is impossible to verify the theories of Chatzigiakoumis 229ff about the linguistic modifications in the *Belthandros* text on our present knowledge of 15th century Greek. He says that the text as it is cannot be much older than the 15th century, and we strongly doubt whether this can be substantiated.

[140] On the possibility of a shortening see Agapitos, *Narrative Structure* 68-70 and 149-154, on discoursive correctness, *ibid*. 167-170.

[141] Pichard's edition of the *Kallimachos* is not very reliable, see Chatzigiakoumis 177-178 and P. A. Agapitos, 'Textkritisches zu *Kallimachos und Chrysorrhoe*', Ελληνικά 41 (1990) 33-41.

greatest objections to Beaton's book lies. We do not disagree with the idea of writing a comprehensive account of the Byzantine romances, primarily designed for non-specialists, but we strongly object to doing it in such a way that it will look as if basic editorial problems were already solved and could be dismissed and set aside to be treated by historians of Byzantine studies.

Now in the case of *Livistros* there is no way out. We have five manuscripts that cannot possibly be construed into a stemma. No original can be reconstructed on the basis of what we have here, none of the manuscripts can be said to reflect in a more reliable way than the others a lost original version of the romance. All of them are different (but not in the sequence of plot-elements, we would add, contrary to what Beaton says [102]) though it is possible to establish groups of manuscripts. Lambert's edition is basically a synoptic text of the Escorial MS on the left-hand pages and a composite text based on the Leyden and Naples MSS on the right-hand pages.[142] After the discovery of the Vatican manuscript, *Vat. gr.* 2391,[143] the problem is even more complicated, since this witness is highly idiosyncratic. It should be stressed that whatever changes have been made in the Vatican version, they must have happened in a lost ancestor. There are no signs in the MS of the scribe making any changes as against his *Vorlage*. It becomes obvious that what we have here in the MSS of *Livistros*, are five different versions that cannot be reconciled, but have to be presented as different texts, as different realizations of the same story. This is also the situation in the *Achilleid*, at least when we compare the Oxford version to the Naples and London versions. It seems that Beaton has not realized the complications and the consequences for his view of the romances. For he proposes that pending a new critical edition, the 'best way to read this romance is to follow the right hand pages of Lambert's edition, crossing over to the left wherever a gap appears on the right' (103). In that case the reader will be reading a 'story that never was', a combination of several versions that certainly never existed anywhere.[144]

The situation prevailing in the *Livistros*, we submit, is not a unique and particularly complex one. It is rather what we have to a greater or lesser degree in all

---

[142] J.A. Lambert, *Le roman de Libistros et Rhodamné publié d'apres les manuscrits de Leyde et de Madrid avec une introduction, des observations grammaticales et un glossaire* (Amsterdam 1935).

[143] *Pace* Beaton, the Vatican manuscript was not described in 1948; Mercati presented the discovery in a still unpublished paper at the 7th Byzantine Congress, and no description was given until Chatzigiakoumis in 1977.

[144] For a detailed discussion of the editorial problems in the *Livistros*, see now P. A. Agapitos '*Libistros und Rhodamne*: Vorläufiges zu einer kritischen Ausgabe der Version A', JÖB 42 (1992) [forthcoming]. The Vatican version has now been edited by Tina Lendari in her Cambridge thesis.

our vernacular texts transmitted in more than one MS. And it will not do to lay the blame for this on the scribes and suspect their *studium novandi* to have been at work. There is no evidence at all that scribes interfered with the texts in the way presupposed by most scholars.

Finally, the *Byzantine Iliad* is said to be the latest of the original romances for no better reasons, it seems, than a supposedly greater percentage of presumedly direct borrowings from other texts, and 'a significant number of Italian loan-words'. Until such statements be quantified and statistics set out, we would doubt the validity of this kind of more or less subjective arguments.[145] There is also a chronological problem which Beaton does not discuss. If, as we have seen above, the Trojan end of the **N** *Achilleid* is regarded as interpolated from the *Byzantine Iliad*, it will not do to say as Beaton does (104) that the *Byzantine Iliad* should be assigned to a date between the mid-fifteenth and the mid-sixteenth centuries. On this theory, which we do not accept, the *Byzantine Iliad* necessarily must be dated before the writing of the Naples MS of the *Achilleid*, that is *before* the last quarter of the fifteenth century. But this only goes to show that you cannot have your cake and eat it.

The problem of the relation between the end of the **N** *Achilleid* and the *Byzantine Iliad* is as follows: the Naples version ends with a Trojan Achilles, as the *Byzantine Iliad* does. Moreover, there are close verbal similarities between the two texts, so that the *Byzantine Iliad* often has been described as interpolated from the *Achilleid*. We do not want to accept such reasoning, but would rather see a significant point in the parallel developments of the two poems, the combination between a medieval heroic poem and a Homeric tradition. Far from being an indication of mutual dependence, this close similarity in structure should be viewed as an indication of a generic relationship.[146]

We would agree with the verdict of Renata Lavagnini who in her close analysis of the textual relationship arrives at the conclusion that 'L'Achilleide non può dunque dipendere dalla Διήγησις del Suppl. gr. 926 [the *Byz. Iliad*], ma nemmeno si può dire il contrario'.[147] And we would also point out the validity for the *Byzantine Iliad* of her conclusion about the end of the *Achilleid*, namely that one could say that the Naples text is

---

[145] See now the detailed discussions of the sources of the *Byzantine Iliad* in Renata Lavagnini's translation and commentary quoted above n. 128.

[146] These problems will be discussed by Ole L. Smith in his forthcoming study of the versions of the *Achilleid*.

[147] *Op.cit.* 84.

'rehomerized' ('riomerizzata') - which is a wholly different judgment than the offhand characterization of the end as an interpolation. In the same way the story of Paris returns to its Homeric setting.

The Stories

One should think that it would be a fairly straightforward and non-controversial affair to give a *précis* of the stories. However, the specialist reader will more than once rub his eyes at Beaton's recounting. Before we comment upon the single romances there is a general point raised in the introductory section (105-106) which must be dealt with first. Beaton notes that in the later romances - as against those of the 12th century - the taboo on sex before marriage 'is flouted, frequently with gusto'. One should think this change was sufficiently important to demand a discussion: why this change, how should it be interpreted? But we are only told that 'in this there may well be a deliberate throwback to the oldest surviving Hellenistic romance, Chariton's *Chaireas and Kallirhoe*, in which the lovers *are married* at the beginning and then experience a series of trials before they can be reunited' (106, our emphasis). It is not clear to us what this is meant to explain (irrespective of whether one would accept an explanation of this kind), since we are talking about pre-marital sex. The whole question of sexuality and sexual relations in the romances should be discussed in some more detail than this.[148]

It is instructive to notice that the two romances that get away more or less unscathed from Beaton's retelling, are the two most well known, *Kallimachos* and *Belthandros*. There are only one or two minor points, such as, e.g., his placing Tarsos at the coast (cf. *Belth.* 235) and the 'swimming-pool' in *Kallimachos* which can only call

---

[148] In a recent article Lynda Garland, '"Be Amorous, But Be Chaste...": Sexual Morality in Byzantine Learned and Vernacular Romance', BMGS 14 (1990) 62-120 discusses at length the sexual *mores* and the attitude of the romance's characters to sexual behaviour. There are certain positions of the author with which we agree and others with which we disagree. One point, though, has to be made, a point which holds good for Beaton's work as well: there is a marked lack of knowledge of the historical/social processes during Byzantine times and a lack of familiarity with Byzantine culture and its literary products. This approach must necessarily lead to a peculiarly one-sided presentation of the romances' position in their socio-cultural context, which leaves the knowledgeable scholar unconvinced. For some tentative assessments see the abstracts of our papers in J. Tatum - Gail M. Vernazza (ed.), *The Ancient Novel. Classical Paradigms and Modern Perspectives*. Proceedings of the 2nd International Conference on the Ancient Novel [Dartmouth College, 23-29 July 1989] (Hanover, N. H. 1990) 121-122; furthermore Agapitos, ClMed 41 (1990) 268-270; H.-G. Beck, 'Ortodossia ed erotismo. Marginalia alla letteratura erotica bizantina', in: H.-G. Beck - F. Conca - Carolina Cupane, *Il romanzo tra cultura latina e cultura bizantina*. Testi della III settimana residenziale di studi medievali (Carini, Villa Belvedere, 17-21 Ottobre 1983), a cura di C. Roccaro [Biblioteca del' Enchiridion 5] (Palermo 1986) 13-32 and *id.*, *Byzantinisches Erotikon* (München 1986).

forth some grave misconceptions with the non-specialist. In *Livistros* the problems become more serious. Livistros does certainly not shoot his arrows through the window into Rhodamni's bedchamber (111 and repeated 157). They do not make love before the marriage, at least the text here (**E** 2214f) is open to interpretation.[149] And most important, there is no indication in the *Livistros* text that Klitovos by telling the story is trying to regain Myrtane's favours (112 and again 123, 125, 188). This mistaken plot-element is then used by Beaton to support his *psychological* interpretation of Klitovos' omission in his narration to Livistros of Myrtane's helping him escape from prison, while revealing it to Rhodamni later on: 'By delaying the revelation to his fictional audience, which includes Myrtane herself, of his mistress' active role in saving his life, he also places his affirmation of gratitude closer to the time when the narrative will, according to its own fiction, come to an end and the narrator can be expected to claim his reward from Myrtane' (125-126). The danger of offering 'psychological' interpretations for the structural devices of a work based on imitative compositional principles becomes obvious. There is no question in the romance about the more explicit, down-to-earth relation between Myrtane and Klitovos. In fact, he is 'brazen' enough to narrate to Myrtane his marriage with Rhodamni's sister and their happy years in Argyrokastron. No psychological subtlety is involved here, nor is any asked for by author and reader.

In the *Achilleid* one begins to have doubts as to whether Beaton has read the texts carefully enough. He does not mention the important point that Pandrouklos warns Achilles of the power of love (**N** 283-298), and that he afterwards reminds Achilles of his warning (1045-1047) which is the main feature that keeps the plot together. The point of Achilles having a picture of Eros made is to invoke the help of Eros to make the girl fall in love with him. Achilles' second visit to the girl is not 'a more formal visit' but their exchange of the symbol of marriage, which is also why Achilles can abduct her the following night. His stroke at the wall of the bedchamber is not an earnest of his sincerity, nor does he say so. There is a much more obvious explanation of Achilles' destruction of this well known symbol of the girl's virginity. It is here enough to point out that according to the text Achilles' feat is carried out with his ἐρωτικὸ ἀπελατίκι (1195), a plain double entendre, if there ever was one.[150] At the tournament after the formal marriage ceremonies, Pandrouklos does not distinguish himself (*pace* Beaton), rather the opposite, since Achilles in a central episode (not mentioned by Beaton), which

---

[149] See the exposition of the problem in Agapitos, *Narrative Structure* 291 n. 52.

[150] See Ole L. Smith's forthcoming paper from the Dartmouth conference (cf. above n. 148) to be published in Ἑλληνικά 42 (1991).

illuminates Achilles' unstable temper (he threatens to kill his wife for her lack of confidence in his strength), has to make good Pandrouklos' defeat at the hands of the Frankish knight who crashes the party, so to speak, and joins the tournament.

It is the *Byzantine Iliad* that gets the worst treatment. Until Paris' flight from Troy the summary is fair enough, except that Beaton represents Paris as setting out for adventure, whereas in the text he is escaping from his fellow Trojans who try to get rid of him by burning the tower in which he is locked up (391-392). He is then shipwrecked and saved on to an island where some monks take care of him (442ff). We change to Helen and are told how all kings are fighting to win her (503ff, 520-521). There is nothing in the text to support Beaton's description that 'she keeps vigil in a lonely castle[151] on another island[152] and all the heroes of the world are engaged in a tournament to win her' (113). Menelaos is said by Beaton to prevail - but according to the text what happens is that the kings finally prefer to throw lots instead of making war (530).[153] Having thus won Helen, Menelaos has the other kings swear to assist him if someone should run away with her. We then change back to Paris with the monks on the island. He makes inquiries about the country, and on hearing of Menelaos and Helen who are looking for brave knights he decides to try his luck there (590ff). He enters the castle and throws away the frock the monks gave him (there is no question about him entering the castle in disguise as a monk as Beaton repeatedly claims[154]), and his natural beauty appears in spite of his poor clothes (615f). We then hear about his excellence in serving Menelaos, and how Helen falls in love with him (661ff). They keep a love affair going in secret and when Menelaos wants to go away to see one of his castles, Paris is given command at home. In Beaton (p.113) all this is described thus: 'no sooner is he (i.e. Menelaos) married to her than he has, conveniently, to depart on an expedition. Paris, in the guise of his monastic hosts, succeeds in entering the castle, and then throws off his disguise to impress the retainers there by his courtly bearing and feats of arms. He at once falls in love with Helen ...' In fact, he does not, it takes some time, and in the text it is Helen that is first said to fall in love with Paris.

---

[151] At l. 533 her father is mentioned, so she cannot be wholly left alone?

[152] There is nothing in the text to suggest an island.

[153] The same error is made by Beaton again later on (156) where he once again represents Helen's castle as being 'besieged by all the eligible princes of the world, who fight tournaments to determine who is to win the owner as his bride'. By the way, Helen is not the 'owner' of the castle.

[154] See also Beaton 158. In this latter passage a number of other points in the texts have been misunderstood to suit the particular purpose of highlighting the castle motif. Achilles, for instance, does not subdue 'a sumptuous castle by force'.

The remaining part of the romance is retold with fewer mistakes but we would submit that the extraordinary errors already committed makes the reader doubt how familiar Beaton is with the text he describes.

Chapter 9

Translations and adaptations of Western romances

Beaton believes (132) that the first Western romance to be translated into vernacular Greek was the voluminous poem *Roman de Troie* by Benoît de St.Maure, probably done around 1350.[155] We have no means of knowing why this particular text was selected, though we cannot exclude the possibility that its Greek theme made it attractive.

In his discussion of the translated Western texts Beaton attempts to make this possibility into a general theory: the Western texts that were translated into vernacular Greek in Byzantium were chosen for their Greek thematic origin or their similarity to the particular plot-structure of the Greek romance (132). We have no evidence that this was so, and only in one of the cases of a Greek translation of a Western romance do we have some indication why it was selected. Boccaccio's *Theseid,* though hardly a romance at all, attracted the attention of a Venetian Greek press;[156] the number of Italian MSS and editions suggests that is was a very widely read text. Probably it was brought out in the Greek translation mainly because of the success of the Italian chapbook edition of the poem published in Venice some time before the Greek text appeared.[157] This latter point cannot be proved, of course, but seems to us to make sense. Against Beaton's theory it must be said that the Greek connection of a text like *Florios and Platziaflore* is difficult to see, apart from the similarity to the general plot-structure of the Greek romances. If this similarity is to be accepted as a sufficient criterium, it should be made clear to the reader that the plot-structure of the *Florios* is not different from that of other Western romances. In fact, what Beaton construes as a typical Greek plot, seems to us to be nothing especially Greek, and in any case cannot be used as proof for this principle of selection.

The *War of Troy* is found in a relatively large number of MSS, and according to its prospective editors, it is possible to establish an acceptable *stemma codicum.*[158] It seems

---

[155] He does so by referring to Elizabeth Jeffreys, 'The Manuscripts and Sources of the War of Troy'. *Actes du XIVe Congrès international des études byzantines* (Bucarest 1971) 91-94, although it appears from her paper that there is no real evidence for this early date at all. The MSS of the Greek text take us no further back than the middle of the 15th century, though it is uncertain whether even this can be substantiated. We have seen no solid evidence for the dating of the oldest MSS.

[156] The press of Nicolini da Sabio, cf. Follieri, 'Su alcuni libri' 136 (below n. 176).

[157] Cf. Birgit Olsen, ClMed 41 (1990) 276f.

[158] Jeffreys and Jeffreys, *Okeanos* 316.

prudent, however, to withhold judgment on this point until the edition has appeared, for if the editors are right, this text would be the only one transmitted in more than one manuscript, where the construction of a *stemma* is possible. From what has appeared in published articles by the editors we do not feel convinced that a stemma has more than a symbolic value in this case.[159]

Like the prospective editors, Beaton also points out that the number of surviving MSS containing the *War of Troy* is extraordinary and would indicate that the text despite its length enjoyed a certain popularity. The problem is, however, how old the seven MSS are and where they were written. As far as one can judge from the slender information available, at least some of the MSS were written in Italy - none of them, as far as we are aware, can be dated with certainty before 1453. Two of them might just be earlier than the fall of Constantinople, the majority are from the 16th century and thus prove absolutely nothing. They may all have been produced for the MS trade.

To make this point clear once and for all. The number of extant MSS of a given work can prove popularity only if they appear in either massive quantity within a relatively limited period or with an even distribution over a long period of time. *Vice versa*, the work preserved in a *codex unicus* cannot be characterized as unpopular if its reception can be demonstrated in contemporary and later texts. There are some good examples from learned Byzantine literature to illustrate the points. Makrembolites' text, is now known from over 40 MSS (admittedly some of these carry only a portion of the romance) but only three are older than the 15th century.[160] This, *prima facie*, shows only that the work was of particular interest for scholars and collectors after the fall of the Empire, but it proves nothing about Byzantine readership. On the other hand, the even distribution of MSS preserving the works of Gregorios Nazianzenos from the late 9th century onwards demonstrates clearly the Cappadocian Father's popularity among Byzantine readers.[161] Finally, Psellos' *Chronographia* is preserved in a single MS (*Par. gr.* 1712); however, the work is quoted more than once *verbatim* by 12th century

---

[159] The stemma given in Elizabeth Jeffreys' paper on the MSS is highly problematic in that the stemmatically best MSS **A** and **X** in practice have no better value for the text than the MSS in inferior stemmatical position. See also the remarks of M. Papathomopoulos in: H. Eideneier (ed.), *Neograeca Medii Aevi* 279ff. For some remarks on this mistaken use of stemma, see below p. 100f. On the *War of Troy* see also A. Z. di Benedetto, Siculorum Gymnasium 30 (1977) 225-244.

[160] For the MSS of Makrembolites, see Annaclara Cataldi Palau, 'La tradition manuscrite d' Eustathe Makrembolitès', Revue d'Histoire de Textes 10 (1980) 75-113.

[161] On the complex transmission of Gregorios' works see P. Gallay, *Les manuscrits des Lettres de Saint Grégoire de Nazianze* (Paris 1957), H. M. Wehrhahn, *Übersichtstabellen zur handschriftlichen Überlieferung der Gedichte Gregors von Nazianz* (Aachen 1967) and the edition of Gregorios' orations in the *Sources Chrétiennes* (Paris 1980ff).

historians like Nikephoros Bryennios, Anna Komnene and Ioannes Skylitzes, which demonstrates its popularity at least with literati at the imperial court.[162] The highest caution, therefore, is necessary when using the manuscripts for such purposes without putting them into their appropriate socio-historical context. It must also be emphasized that no useful conclusions can be drawn from such an insignificant number of MSS as seven. Certainly, in comparison with the other vernacular texts we are dealing with here, the number is extraordinary; the problem is that we have no means of knowing whether this number is really significant or whether it is just an accident. But since there are many other texts transmitted in much larger numbers of MSS, we should be extremely wary in assessing the popularity or dissemination of the vernacular texts on such slender evidence.[163]

In the case of the *Florios*[164] it seems almost impossible to make sense of the relation between the two MSS, the Vienna *theol. gr.* 244 and the London, British Museum *Add.* 8241.[165] Beaton does not touch this point at all, and to judge from his discussion there is no problem. He does not even mention the MSS. He refers to Kriaras[166] for the probable date of the Greek translation, but it is obvious from Kriaras that the latter had nothing to go upon except for the *terminus post* given by the Tuscan original (first half of

---

[162] On Bryennios and Skylitzes see the respective editions by Gautier and Thurn in the CFHB. On Komnene see St. Linnér, 'Psellus' Chronographia and the Alexias', BZ 76 (1983) 1-9 and E. V. Maltese, 'Anna Comnena nel mare delle sventure (Alex. xiv 7,4)', BZ 80 (1987) 1-2.

[163] No doubt it is significant that, e.g., Hero's treatise *Pneumatica* can be found in a large number of MSS from the 16th century, see W. Schmidt, *Heronis Alexandrini Opera Quae Supersunt Omnia vol. i. Supplementum. Die Geschichte der Textüberlieferung* (Leipzig 1899). This text (and other similar technical treatises) caught the attention of an age and a public interested in the scientific aspects and attainments of Antiquity.

[164] Most of the relevant literature on this text can be found in G. Spadaro's *Contributo sulle fonti del romanzo greco-medievale 'Florio e Plaziaflora'* [Κείμενα καὶ μελέται νεοελληνικῆς φιλολογίας 26] (Athens 1966).

[165] As is well known the London MS **L** is lacunose at the beginning of the *Achilleid* text. The loss of text, however, may be used to reconstruct at least one earlier stage: the loss of lines 1-14 may be explained from **L** itself, since the scribe writes 10 lines to a page, the title and the first 14 lines may have been on a first folio now lost in **L**. It appears from Haag (cf. above n. 125) 13 that Krumbacher found that one page had been torn out (he was still able to see the remains) from **L** before the first page containing the *Florios* (f.78), and with this lost page ff. 78-84 make up a gathering. There is on f. 84v a *reclamatio* that proves the point. Further, it also becomes clear in this way that the *Florios* was contained in a separate MS and bound together with the *Achilleid*. But after line 15 there is in **L** a note in red ink λείπει ἐδῶ which must mean that the scribe of **L**'s Vorlage was able to see from his exemplar that some portion of text was missing here. Obviously the note came from the MS that **L** was copying; the scribe of **L** left room for a note here to be written in red ink (f. 78r). The loss of lines 16-35 in an ancestor of **L** can be explained by assuming a similar format for this ancestor as for **L** with ca. 10 lines to a page.

[166] *Βυζαντινὰ ἱπποτικὰ μυθιστορήματα* [Βασικὴ βιβλιοθήκη 2] (Athens 1955) 139.

the 14th century) and the *terminus ante* of the date of the two Greek MSS.[167]

Anyone who takes a look at the apparatus in Kriaras' edition will notice the great differences between the two MSS.[168] In fact, the differences are so extensive that one would have to assume several intermediate stages between an original translation and the extant MSS in order to account for the development of their diverse character. To mention but one of the characteristic differences: L contains some subtitles in prose written in red ink which cannot have been part of the original Tuscan text, but on the other hand it is a feature found in several of the original Greek romances. For example after l. 63 on f. 79r there is a subtitle ἔφερον καὶ παρέδωκάν την εἰς τὸν βασιλέα. and again on f. 81v after l.110 (not 109 as Kriaras says) κάθεται ὁ βασιλεὺς καὶ ἡ βασίλισσα νὰ παρηγοροῦν τὴν κόρην.[169] We have no doubt that the presence of this feature in L points to the red ink subtitles as integral parts of the vernacular romances, and not as later additions by 'monkish scribes' or 'diaskeuasts'. In fact, we have never seen any convincing argument offered that the rubrics found in almost all vernacular romances (*Belthandros* being the notable exception) could not be part of the original composition. Some of the 'additions' in V in Kriaras' apparatus are undoubtedly also such subtitles but

---

[167] Beaton says with reference to Kriaras' edition 139 that the date of the translation is generally thought to lie within the second half of the 14th century or at the latest the early years of the 15th century. Kriaras does not say so here, but gives the date 'end of 14th or beginning of 15th century'. In his paper at the 1958 Byzantine congress in Munich ('Die zeitliche Einreihung des Phlorios und Platzia-Phlora'-Romans in Hinblick auf den 'Imberios und Margarona'-Roman', *Akten des XI. internationalen Byzantinistenkongresses München 1958* [München 1960] 269) Kriaras gave the date as in Beaton. Kriaras 139 has no certain date for the London MS (2nd half of the 15th century) and dates erroneously the Vienna MS at around 1550. This is unfortunately characteristic of Beaton's dealing with his sources on such questions. We need a lot more precision in these matters, and must distinguish between exact information and more or less rough guesses. It makes some difference whether the translation can be dated with certainty before 1453. It cannot, however, be thus dated, for at present we have no definite date for the London MS which is the older of the two. L cannot be easily analysed for watermarks due to the binding, and the date most often given, the second half of the 15th century (cf. e.g. H.-G. Beck, *Geschichte der Textüberlieferung* 480; G. Spadaro, Byzantion 33 [1963] 455 n. 2; Kriaras 139) rests on no better evidence than Hesseling's view of the script (*L'Achilleide byzantine* 17). The old British Museum catalogue says '16th century' which we regard as much too late. On the question of the date of V it is interesting that the date of mid-16th century usually given in older literature, derives from Sathas who knew that the book had belonged to Busbeck and thought that it was contemporary with the latter's stay in Constantinople from 1554-1562 as Ambassador. That no one questioned this faulty reasoning shows that not many scholars saw the MS, and if they did they can have had no idea of palaeography. Cf. also below n. 233.

[168] It must be noted here, however, that Kriaras' apparatus is not as trustworthy as one could wish. Especially L has not been reported with the necessary precision. On his collation of V there are a few critical remarks by G. Spadaro in BZ 67 (1974) 69ff.

[169] For further examples see, e.g., f. 118r (after l. 832) and f. 129r (after l. 1048) from both of which appears that the rubrics were entered after the main text had been written.

in this MS they are totally different and appear at other points than in L; they have received no special status and have been integrated in the text. On f. 216r after 788 there is no doubt that the prose passage βούλεται ὁ αὐθέντης τοῦ τόπου βουλὴν τοιαύτην is a subtitle though it is not distinguished as such in the text. We may add here on the question of the rubrics that in the *Livistros* they are all in verse, whereas in the other romances we find both verse and prose rubrics. In the *Byzantine Iliad* two of the rubrics show that they cannot be regarded as additions; they are organic part of the text, for they are necessary to the understanding of the text (*Byz.Il.* 202 and 257). Also it must be stressed that Hesseling's idea that the rubrics in the London MS of the *Florios* pointed towards an illustrated MS cannot be substantiated. [170]

The neatness of Kriaras' text of the *Florios* is deceptive; it does not make the reader aware of the wide divergencies between the two manuscripts (or dare we say 'versions'?) which appear as soon as one looks into the apparatus. Then it becomes clear that Kriaras' text is an attempt at a reconstruction of a presumed archetypus made out of two incompatible witnesses. We think that there is a case for a reconsideration of the problem of the 'translations', for when we get to the *Imberios* no sane person would for one moment consider the idea of a translation, while the manuscripts of the *Imberios* do not behave more orderly than did those of the *Florios*.

Beaton claims that the *Florios* is a 'fairly close translation of the well-known late medieval story of *Fleur and Blanchefleur*' (134). There is no reference to the discussion of whether we have the model on which the translation was based[171], nor are we given any arguments for the view that we have to do with a 'fairly close translation'. Anyone who cares to take a look into the Tuscan text which is commonly believed to have been the model (at least this is accepted by Beaton) will find that the Greek text is not a translation; it is an adaptation, and perhaps even a close one, but in no sense a translation.[172]

Nor is the similar problem in the *Imberios* dealt with at all by Beaton, who refers

---

[170] *Le roman de Phlorios et Platzia Phlore, publié avec une introduction, des observations et un index* par D. C. Hesseling [Verhandlingen der Koninklijke Akademie van Wetenschappen te Amsterdam, Afdeeling Letterkunde, N.R. xvii 4] (Amsterdam 1917) 18. So far no illustrated MS of Byzantine vernacular literature has been found at all. For the single miniature extant and preserved, in the *Scalig.* 55 of *Livistros* see Agapitos, *Narrative Structure* 24 n. 17. The printed edition of Loukanis' *Iliad* (Venice 1526) is a wholly different matter.

[171] For the controversy between Schreiner and Spadaro, see the latter's *Contributo* (quoted above n. 164).

[172] We are not convinced by Spadaro who argues (*op.cit.*) for the Tuscan text that we have as the source; nor do we agree with Schreiner who wanted to put a common source for the Tuscan and the Greek text. On Spadaro's theory, the translator either used several MSS or a MS liberally supplied with variant readings; such a MS probably never existed.

to the article on the *Imberios* by Elizabeth and Michael Jeffreys.[173] The main interest of Beaton is again the presumed motives for the selection of this text to be translated (136). To see this in the all too common plot-structure (meeting of the lovers, separation, reunion) as particularly appealing to a Greek translator (who would recognize this structure in the common stock of the Greek romances from Chariton on) is to build too much on slippery ground. We are not convinced that the Western romances translated were so different from other Western romances that we need this Greekness as a special reason for their being selected for a Greek audience.

Also in the case of the *Imberios* we are told that it must have enjoyed popularity judging from the number of extant manuscripts. None of these can be dated before 1453, and three of them may for all we know have been written in Italy.[174]

The *Theseid* has been neglected by investigators and editors, though there is now hope that we may have a modern edition.[175] Beaton is probably right in saying that this translation was made in Western territory. We do not think that the case for Crete as the geographical setting is very strong, and the evidence does not permit Beaton's further conclusion that the *Theseid* translation shows that the Palaiologian romances were known in Crete. It is much more likely that the translation was made in Venice.

As was first shown by Enrica Follieri and David Holton the very MS from which the 1529 φυλλάδιο was printed is the *Vat. Pal. gr.* 426 probably written by Dimitrios

---

[173] 'Imberios and Margarona: the manuscripts, sources and edition of a Byzantine verse romance', Byzantion 41 (1971) 122-160. We agree with the criticism raised here of Kriaras' edition which prints a text that never was - an impossible mixture of readings from the different manuscripts. There is much to recommend in the procedure proposed by the Jeffreys: to print basically the text of **N** and give the readings of the other MSS in the apparatus if one does not prefer to present the versions synoptically.

[174] The MSS are **V**, Vienna *theol. gr.* 244; **N,** Napoli iii. B. 27; **H** and **G** both in *Vat. Pal. gr.* 426; and **O**, Oxford, Bodleian Library *misc.* 287. Of these perhaps **O** and **V** were written in Greece to judge from the owners' notes. *Vat. Pal. gr.* 426 was written in Venice in the third decade of the 16th century, and for the Naples codex, see above n. 123.

[175] An edition is being prepared by Birgit Olsen, cf. her paper 'The Greek Translation of Boccaccio's Theseid Book 6', ClMed 41 (1990) 273-301 where she presents a preliminary text of Book 6. Until now we have only had an edition of Book I by E. Follieri, *Il Teseida Neogreco. Libro I.* Saggio di edizione [Testi e Studi Bizantino-Neoellenici I. Collezione diretta da C. Gianelli e G. Zoras] (Istituto di Studi Bizantini, Università di Roma, Roma-Atene 1959).

Zinos,[176] who has also entered his corrections in the MS and thus gives us a unique glimpse into the working processes of the scholar preparing a vernacular text for the printer.[177] It is still not certain whether the *Vat. Pal. gr.* 426 is a direct copy from the other surviving MS of the text, *Par. gr.* 2898.[178] If, as is very likely, Zinos prepared his MS on the basis of the actual Paris MS or a MS very close to it, he may already have changed the text of his *Vorlage* when writing out the 'first state' of the MS destined to be the printer's copy, as was suggested by Follieri. He then made the changes and additions appearing as such in *Vat. Pal. gr.* 426. If this is a correct diagnosis of Zinos' work on the

---

[176] Follieri in her studies 'La versione in greco volgare del Teseida del Boccaccio', *Atti dell' VIII Congresso internazionale di studi bizantini* (Roma 1953) 67-77, especially pp. 70ff, and 'Su alcuni libri greci stampati a Venezia nella prima metà del cinquecento', *Contributi alla storia del libro italiano. Miscellanea in onore di Lamberto Donati* (Firenze 1969) 119-164, especially 136-145, showed that the Vatican MS had been used for the edition of the *Theseid*. Then, in his edition of the Alexander romance, David Holton argued that the scribe and subsequent corrector of the Vatican was Dimitrios Zinos whose hand was known from the subscribed MS *Esc.* T.ii.18 (See Διήγησις τοῦ Ἀλεξάνδρου. *The Tale of Alexander. The Rhymed Version*. Critical edition with an introduction and commentary by David Holton [Βυζαντινὴ καὶ νεοελληνικὴ βιβλιοθήκη 1] [Thessaloniki 1974] 46 n. 5). Follieri agreed with this identification in her paper 'Il libro greco per i Greci nelle imprese editoriali romane e veneziane della prima metà del cinquecento', *Venezia centro di mediazione tra oriente e occidente (secoli xv-xvi). Aspetti e problemi* (Firenze 1977) 490 (see also Linos Politis' accept in his paper ['Venezia come centro della stampa e della diffusione della prima letteratura neoellenica'] in the same volume p.462), and no one has, as far as we know, questioned this judgment. However, the case is far from as clear-cut as is commonly believed. First, we do not have any autograph subscription by Zinos; the subscription in the Escorial MS is by another hand (see Ernst Gamillscheg-Dieter Harlfinger, *Repertorium der griechischen Kopisten 800-1600. 1. Grossbritannien. A. Verzeichnis der Kopisten* [Wien 1981] 94; by the way, there is no reference in the *Repertorium* to the Vatican MS). Further, as Birgit Olsen has pointed out to us, there are some important differences in *ductus* between the hand represented on plate 94 in the *Repertorium* (from the Escorial MS) and the hand found in the Vatican MS. At least it is very likely that he was the responsible editor for the book, given his association with the publishers, see Follieri, 'Il libro greco' 491ff. On Zinos in general see Holton, *op.cit.* 43-46.

[177] See Follieri's paper 'Su alcuni libri' referred to in the preceding note. There is nothing on the MSS in Beaton. For the *Theseid* part of the Paris MS see Birgit Olsen, *op.cit.* 279 who has shown on the basis of the watermarks that at least this part of the Paris MS should be dated c. 1500. For the hands in the Paris MS see note 96 above. Beck, 'Leserkreis' 64 took up the question whether *Vat. Pal. gr.* 426 had been also in the case of the *Imberios* the source for the φυλλάδιο. This is not very likely, for this part of the MS lacks the various notes for the typesetter found in the *Theseid*. But see H. Schreiner, 'Der älteste Imberiostext', *Akten des XI. internationalen Byzantinistenkongresses* (München 1960) 558-559. See also on the *Imberios* MSS Elizabeth Jeffreys, 'Some Comments on the Manuscripts of *Imberios and Margarona*', Ἑλληνικά 27 (1974) 39-49. She does not comment on Schreiner's idea, but suggests that *Vat. Pal. gr.* 426 may have connection with an earlier printed *Imberios* edition than the 1553 one usually regarded as the *editio princeps*.

[178] Birgit Olsen, *op. cit.* 277 has pointed out that there is a case for regarding the Vatican MS as a copy of the Paris MS. We are indebted to her for information and suggestions regarding the case of the *Theseid*.

text, there is no reason why we should not envisage the other φυλλάδια as having been produced in the same way. The other texts appearing as chapbooks are very likely to have undergone the same processes of corrections and changes. If this is so, the principles and methods behind Zinos' work in his MS should be studied in detail for the light they may throw on the relation between the edition and the MS text of, e.g., the Απόκοπος. At least one thing seems certain to us: these texts as printed were the result of 'philological' redaction by the editor.[179]

Much space is taken up by Beaton's inability to make up his mind what to do with the idea of the Kahanes that the name Arcita in the *Theseid* was derived from Akritis.[180] As far as we can see there are no good reasons for such an assumption; the whole idea is rather far-fetched and Beaton's indecisive pro et contra does his judgement no credit.

---

[179] The *Alexander Romance* was until the find of the 1509 *Apokopos* the only one of the Venetian chapbooks where the editor (in the epilogue) tells us about his work, see Holton, *op. cit.* 40-43. The whole complex of problems of the *Theseid* and the work of the editor will be studied in detail by Birgit Olsen in a forthcoming paper. On the recently discovered 1509 edition of *Apokopos* see now the splendid study by N. M. Panagiotakis, Τὸ κείμενο τῆς πρώτης ἐκδόσης τοῦ " Ἀπόκοπου". Τυπογραφικὴ καὶ φιλολογικὴ διερεύνηση (Venice 1991). It is strange, however, that Panagiotakis does not squarely face the possibility that Nikolaos Kalliergis, who was responsible for the edition, may have worked in exactly the same way as did Zinos in the *Theseid*. If Kalliergis did so, there is no reason at all to prefer the printed text of 1509 to the MS text in **V**.

[180] Speculum 20 (1945) 415-425.

Chapter 10

Genealogy of the romances

With the opening of this chapter Beaton introduces the reader to some general remarks concerning literary theory, in this case connected specifically with the question of a text's relation to earlier and later works. We have already pointed out (see above p. 13f) that Beaton's approach to literary theory is problematic. Just as he remains on the surface of available studies for the historical questions, so does he remain on the surface of the ever-growing bibliography on theoretical approaches to literary criticism. What is most annoying is the incongruence between the theoretical works cited and their actual application in the subsequent analysis. For one thing, Beaton presents his readers with a series of theoreticians ranging from T. S. Eliot to Roland Barthes from whose works he 'draws broadly' (143) to establish his view of textual relations. As a result it remains unclear what exactly the term 'intertextuality' means for him. The key to the problem once again lies in his hiding under a cloak of references to modern literary theory a conventional (and surely not 'rigorously historical' [*ibid.*]) interpretation. This is blatantly revealed when he states that 'the consonance between the Byzantines own view of mimesis, discussed in Chapter 2 and aspects of the modern theories should also be born in mind' (143). In what way does the Byzantine notion of *mimesis* correlate to theories of intertextuality? *Prima facie*, we would say: none! None, because the approaches to the relation of texts to each other are governed in the two cases by completely different sets of rules and aesthetic conventions. It is therefore necessary first to clarify exactly what intertextuality means and how modern theoreticians use it. Then one should oppose this concept to various medieval texts and see how they function. It would be seen, and this we have already demonstrated in our criticism of Chapter 2, that in most cases the evidence is tenuous and highly subjective, because the analysis operates on the level of assumed *clichées* (be it for modern theory or medieval works) rather than on an in-depth knowledge of the actual texts.

Beaton proceeds to suggest that his approach to the texts is 'genealogical'. This term is explained by a reference to Hans Robert Jauss, suggesting that with this term we avoid the notion of influence and show the true relationship between two texts: the earlier remains inert until activated by the later. The observation of the German critic is indeed a most valid one, only it has nothing to do with genealogy, a notion that Jauss justly rejects, as he rejects the notion of conventional literary history.[181] Jauss' general framework has been described by him as *Rezeptionsästhetik* and developed both from the analysis of medieval and modern works.[182] Beaton continues his explanation of 'genealogy' as follows:

> 'The metaphor of genealogy, finally, must be understood primarily in the sense of the procedure by which family relationships are retraced and reconstructed, starting out from the present; but at the same time its organic metaphor does not exclude a (metaphorically) 'genetic' reading of literary tradition' (143).

Once again the author uses a technique of ἵξεις ἀφίξεις (to quote the Pythian oracular phrase) in his statement, whereby the reader cannot discern what the author's opinion actually is; in this case, does 'genealogy' mean *Rezeptionsästhetik* or is it a traditional theory of development? The reference (229 n.1) to Paul de Man's essay 'Genesis and genealogy (Nietzsche)'[183] is unfortunate, since it misleads the reader to believe that de Man supports Beaton's views. The whole question, in fact, looks as follows: the concept of a 'genealogy of texts' was discussed by French historians and critics in the sixties on the background of a debate between philosophy and psychology. It was Michel Foucault who formulated most succinctly the Nitzschean concept of genealogy,[184] where genetic metaphors are used but in a seemingly non-evolutionary frame.[185] This idea contrasted strongly to Jacques Derrida's psychological theories about the 'autonomous' text.[186] It is with this debate in mind that Paul de Man wrote his 1972 essay on genealogy and Nietzsche,[187] in which he showed that Nietzsche did very much view the literary text (and,

---

[181] See above p. 18.

[182] See H.R.Jauss, *Ästhetische Erfahrung und literarische Hermeneutik I: Versuche im Feld der ästhetischen Erfahrung* (München 1977) 97-136.

[183] In his *Allegories of reading: Figural language in Rousseau, Nietzsche, Rilke and Proust* (New Haven - London 1979).

[184] As expressed, e.g., in Nietzsche's *Geburt der Tragödie aus dem Geiste der Musik* (1872).

[185] M. Foucault, *Archéologie du savoir* (Paris 1969) and *id.*, 'Nietzsche, généalogie, histoire', in: *Hommage à Jean Hippolite* (Paris 1971) 145-172. Both works have been highly influential, especially among American critics, in the formation of theories on 'genesis' and 'history of texts'; see, for example, the strict application of Foucault's ideas by V. Lambropoulos, *Literature as National Institution. Studies in the politics of Modern Greek Criticism* (Princeton 1988) 23-43 (the chapter is entitled 'Towards a Genealogy of "Literature": The Institutionalization of Tradition in C. Th. Dimaras' *A History of Modern Greek Literature*').

[186] The debate between 'Nietzschean' Foucault and 'Freudian' Derrida has now been ingeniously discussed by L. Ferry - A. Renault, *La pensée 68. Essai sur l'antihumanisme contemporain* (Paris 1988).

[187] 'Genesis and Genealogy in Nietzsche's *Birth of Tragedy*', Diacritics 2.4 (1972) 44-53.

more generally, culture) in a genetic/evolutionary manner. Consequently, de Man's arguments pull away the foundation under Beaton's theoretical construct. Moreover, by quoting de Man's essay in its partly revised version of 1979, Beaton gives a false impression of when and under what circumstances the essay was actually written. Literary theory may partly reject the notion of history, but it is still necessary to see its dialectic progress in its proper historical and scholarly context.

Beaton presents three 'networks of relationships' that according to him have played a role in the genesis and development of the fourteenth and fifteenth-century Greek romances: 'relationships with the older romances (and to a small extent with other texts) in Greek; relationships with the Western medieval romance; and relationships with oral tradition.' (143) The first two are dealt with in this chapter, the third one in the next. The material under consideration is reduced to the 'original' romances, since 'it goes without saying that the genealogy of the translated romances presents far fewer problems' (144). The tripartite division, as well as the reduction of the material demonstrates Beaton's purely subjective and hasty treatment. To suggest that because a text (and let it be stated once again that we are dealing with medieval texts) has been translated it is less open to a 'genealogical' analysis is to misunderstand the whole concept of textual reception and valorization. The analysis of the 'translated' romances has not so far conclusively proven how this whole translation question was handled, and since no stylistic analysis exists we cannot commit ourselves to these generalities. But the tripartite division of genetic development seems to us equally problematic. It is based on a set of *clichées*, which Beaton has wholeheartedly accepted. The valorization of past texts must be seen as a cultural unit which - in the case of the Middle Ages - is held together by the framework of education. It should be pointed out that education does not imply erudition; it suggests a common ground of training which supports a set of cultural notions that interact with the produced literary work of art. To suggest that the author of the *Kallimachos* knew Makrembolites because of the appearance of Eros as a fresco is acceptable only as long as it is taken for what it is worth, namely proving common cultural ground.[188] It is an easy way out to establish flabby notions of 'intertextuality' and then prove the knowledge of texts on tenuous, mostly general motivic, evidence.

Furthermore, why do only the Western romances figure in the second category and not the Eastern - Arabic and Persian - ones? Obviously because no one likes to learn these difficult languages in order to go and read some bad and hard-to-find editions of these works; the familiarity with the Western medieval texts can be considered as given

---

[188] See for a more detailed analysis of these questions Agapitos, *Narrative Structure* 16-19.

for the Western scholar on grounds of actual cultural affinity and/or a Eurocentric point of view, not to mention the far better editions and the availability of commentaries, dictionaries etc. We will discuss the question of oral tradition in the next chapter, but would like to point to the lack of any serious comparative study on the linguistic and thematic similarities between the vernacular romances and Modern Greek folk songs[189] which makes any generalizing statements superficial.

With these questions in mind, we can proceed to look at Beaton's analysis of the 'original' romances in respect to their various 'genealogical' affiliations. And indeed, the first section of the chapter's subdivision entitled 'The twelfth-century and Hellenistic romances' presents us with a deceptive picture of the supposed knowledge of the Palaiologian authors concerning the older works. The expression 'undoubtedly knew' for the author of *Kallimachos* in relation to *Drosilla and Charikles*, *Hysmine and Hysminias*, and (!) the *Aithiopika* is most objectionable. The references to Pichard and Hunger are completely vague[190] without the presentation of a single example (nor is there any in the discussion of the narrative structure of *Kallimachos*). What in Pichard's notes are minor explicative statements, some of them in themselves misleading[191] and what in Hunger are some general remarks, become in Beaton's presentation proven facts concerning textual

---

[189] The study by Promponas (see above n. 52) takes a look at the formulaic structure of *Digenis* **E** and the folk songs with the aim of proving Pontic elements in the text.

[190] 'Pichard 1956: notes passim; Hunger 1968a' (144). Beaton is referring to Hunger's 'Un roman byzantin et son atmosphère: Callimaque et Chrysorrhoé', Travaux et Mémoires 3 (1968) 405-422, reprinted in: *id.*, *Byzantinische Grundlagenforschung* (London 1973).

[191] Pichard 9 n. 1 (similarity in the representation of Charon between *Kal.* and *Dros.*), 17 n. 3 (the petrification effect of the *coupe de foudre* in *Kal.*, *Rhod.* and *Dros.*), 23 n. 1 (hesitation of the heroine to tell her story in *Kal.*, *Hysm.*, *Rhod.*), 27 n. 2 (a wrong reference to *Hysm.* for a supposed similarity between the two phrases), 28 n. 6 (tenuous reference to the 'wing/pen of Aphrodite' in *Kal.* and *Hysm.*), 29 n. 3 (on Graces and bathing in *Kal.*, *Arist.*, *Hysm.*), 30 n. 1 (on *ekphraseis* in the novels and *Kal.*), 30 n. 2 (the ugliness of a monkey as a *tertium comparationis* in *Kal.* and *Hysm.*), 33 n. 4 (night as the traditional hour of the *coup de foudre* in *Kal.*, *Rhod.*, *Hysm.*), 34 n. 2 (the erotic power of the eye as a *topos* in *Kal.*, *Rhod.*, *Dros.*), 37 n. 4 (the isolated hero as a *topos* in *Kal.*, *Rhod.*, *Dros.*), 37 n. 6 (the *locus communis* of erotic dizziness), 51 n. 1 (the motif of the false death), 76 n. 3 (Aphrodite's marriage bed in *Kal.* and *Hysm.*), 86 n. 3 (the hero is defended by the energetic heroine in *Kal.* and Heliod.), 88 n. 4 (narration makes suffering worse in *Kal.*, *Hysm.*, *Dros.*). These are the *passim* notes in Pichard. A quick glance will show that only two references (30 n. 2 and 76 n. 3) could point to a textual reception, and that is specifically of Makrembolites' work. The remaining references are either wrong, tenuous or belong to the category of motivic similarities but not of textual reception; they do not prove that the *Kallimachos*-author used the texts of Heliodoros and the Komnenian novelists.

interaction. The same holds true for *Belthandros*,[192] the *Achilleid*,[193] and the *Byzantine Iliad*.[194] In fact, *Livistros* is the only romance where an exact textual reference can be adduced to support the point that its author might have known other texts and this one Beaton does not mention, although it had been detected by Cupane,[195] and is a series of exempla proving the power of Eros. The fact that the passage appears differently phrased and in varying lengths in Manasses, Eugenianos and Tatios goes to show that direct quotation cannot be assumed. This is a splendid case for Jauss' *Rezeptionsästhetik*, but not for Beaton's 'genealogy'.

What follows is an analysis of points of contact between the Palaiologian and Komnenian works. The main axis of argument lies in the existence of *ekphraseis* in both groups, and the fact that art substitutes nature. As we have argued above p. 41f this simplistic approach cannot stand. Yes, there are *ekphraseis* in the Palaiologian works, but for us they show the power both of genre tradition (one cannot do without them if one composes a romance) and Byzantine education (progymnastic theory being taught throughout). It would have been worthwhile to analyse some of these descriptions in more detail to see how they function in the romances, particularly since there are some interesting structural devices in the later works, which are not to be found in the earlier ones.[196] One particularly intriguing case are the close similarities in various points but with major expansions between Makrembolites and *Livistros*, an indication possibly that *Livistros* is earlier than the other vernacular romances.[197]

We are at a loss with the following examples concerning the rhetorical figures in the Palaiologian authors that supposedly show their knowledge of the earlier works. Beaton produces (146-147) only four examples out of approximately 12.000 verses of the five 'original' romances. In two cases (*Kal.* 449-455 and *Liv.* S 2432-2463)

---

[192] Beaton accepts the Kahanes' 'persuasive argumentation' that *Belthandros* 'is a work of some erudition' (which to us means nothing and proves nothing), but in n. 3 on p. 230 rejects their Narcissus theory which is their main proof of erudition. What remains then of this erudition Beaton has not shown.

[193] See our criticism above p. 53.

[194] On the *Byzantine Iliad* see p.60 above.

[195] "Ἔρως βασιλεύς 257 n. 41 (*Liv.* **N** 161-171 = Konst. Man. *Arist.* fr. 21-21a Mazal = Nik. Eug. *Dros.* iv 135-149 = Ach. Tat. i 17-18).

[196] On the descriptions in the Byzantine romances see the unpublished dissertation by Corinne Jouanno, *L'ekphrasis dans la littérature byzantine d'imagination* (Paris 1987); Bartsch, *Decoding the Ancient Novel* (cf. above n. 89) as well as the important theoretical treatment by Ph. Hamon, *Introduction à l'analyse du descriptif* (Paris 1981); see also *id.*, 'Rhetorical Status of the Descriptive', Yale French Studies 61 (1981) 1-26. On the rhetorical and stylistic use of the descriptive mode in the Palaiologian works, see Agapitos, *Narrative Structure* 177-193.

[197] Some of these points are the narrative frame, the first-person narrator, the frieze descriptions, the imperial imagery of Eros, the 'open' end of the work.

Beaton offers passages so extravagant that any relation with the Komnenian novels must be excluded. It is in fact their length and specific position in the respective works that makes them highly peculiar.[198] Let us look at the example he prints from *Kal.* 449-455. Beaton argues here that the anaphora with a series of parallel phrases is just one of those links with traditional rhetoric. This is true, only such anaphoric cola rarely exceed two sentences (or verses in the case of poetry) as a glance at any work of Byzantine rhetoric can testify.[199] Here is the text:

    Ἐν μέσῳ γάρ - ἀλλὰ πολὺν ὁ λόγος πόνον ἔχει -
450 ἐκ τῶν τριχῶν ἐκρέματο κόρη μεμονωμένη
    - σαλεύει μου τὴν αἴσθησιν, σαλεύει μου τὰς φρένας -
    ἐκ τῶν τριχῶν - αἴ, φρόνημα παράλογον τῆς τύχης -
    ἐκ τῶν τριχῶν ἐκρέματο κόρη - σιγῶ τῷ λόγῳ,
    ἰδοὺ σιγῶ, μετὰ νεκρᾶς καρδίας τοῦτο γράφω -
455 ἐκ τῶν τριχῶν ἐκρέματο κόρη μὲ τῶν χαρίτων·

What is happening here cannot possibly be paralleled from the Komnenian works. The effectiveness of the passage does not lie in the repetition of a phrase (ἐκ τῶν τριχῶν ἐκρέματο κόρη) as Beaton suggests, but in the complex intertwining of authorial interjections with a phrase that contains *the* message of the scene. The repetitions are in fact a double rhetorical figure, the *ekplexis* (surprise) in v.450 which gives full information to the reader (ἐκ τῶν τριχῶν ἐκρέματο κόρη μεμονωμένη) and then a *tricolon abundans* ἐκ τῶν τριχῶν - ἐκ τῶν τριχῶν ἐκρέματο κόρη - ἐκ τῶν τριχῶν ἐκρέματο κόρη μὲ τῶν χαρίτων joined to an inverted *tricolon abundans* of authorial interjections (σαλεύει μου τὴν αἴσθησιν, σαλεύει μου τὰς φρένας - αἴ, φρόνημα παράλογον τῆς τύχης - σιγῶ τῷ λόγῳ). The artistry of the author is indeed great, only it consists of other elements than those seen by Beaton.[200] Similarly superficial is the discussion of the 'wordplay' on ξενοδόχος in *Liv.* **S** 1922-1928, which includes a much

---

[198] The example from *Livistros* is not as Beaton suggests, a direct question, but an indirect one in oblique speech.

[199] As an example we offer the lengthy funerary poem on Maria Skleraina († c.1044/45) by Michael Psellos (see Kurtz-Drexl [Milano 1936] i 190-205 and the recent edition by Maria Dora Spadaro, Catania 1984), where the presence of anaphoric schemata and other rhetorical figures of sound is massive (as it is not in any of the vernacular texts), but never exceeds two verses. For a rare and structurally similar case, see the funerary poem on Theodora Doukaina († ca.1140) by Theodoros Prodromos: τοῦ δεσπότου μου (στῆθί μου, ῥοῦς δακρύων), / τοῦ δεσπότου μου (μὴ ῥαγῇς μοι καρδία), / τοῦ δεσπότου μου (τέτλαθι, στέρνον τάλαν), / τοῦ δεσπότου μου τὴν ὅμευνον καίσαρος (vv. 47-50) in Gautier's edition of Bryennios p. 359.

[200] For a fuller analysis of this passage and similar ones see Agapitos, *Narrative Structure* 87-89.

more complex imagery than Beaton suggests, since ξενοδόχος refers both to the actual innmaster (who is not as is usual a man but a woman, namely Rhodamne as a ξενοδόχισσα) and to the 'heart's innmaster' who is Livistros.²⁰¹

The further links between the 12th and the 14th century works suggested by Beaton (147) belong exactly to those thematic similarities of which there are thousands in Byzantine literature. One could adduce examples for the malevolence of fate, the false death of the hero, and the movement from an early experience to a mature development in all kinds of genres. Does this mean that they have influenced the Palaiologian romances in a 'genealogical' sense? Or can one prove dependence on the Komnenian texts because of these similarities? We would think not, unless exact parallels are present that allow such conclusions. And to prove this point, while showing at the same time how questionable results are produced by the wrong application of literary theory, here follows an example: Gregorios Nazianzenos composed in early 387 a long poem entitled Εἰς τὸν ἑαυτοῦ βίον.²⁰² In this work we can trace all these themes which Beaton sees as links between the romances. Gregorios opens his work with the very concept that his life is a road on which he has trodden towards God (d. v. s. 1-2, 17-20), a theme which runs through the whole work (d. v. s. 277-291, 484-493 [combined with the notion of escape from this path], 728-735, 1146-1152 etc.) expressing a development in spiritual and not psychological terms; he invokes the malevolence and instability of fate (d. v. s. 738-739, 1739); he presents himself as having 'died' twice, once during a storm at sea (d. v. s. 131ff)²⁰³ - here the similarities with the equivalent storm scenes in the romances are most interesting - and the second time metaphorically after his retirement from the episcopal throne of Constantinople (d. v. s. 1919-1949).²⁰⁴ An excellent case, then, to show that both the Komnenian and Palaiologian authors knew this work. This, of course, is neither possible nor necessary. The similarities between Gregorios' poem and the

---

[201] On this passage see Agapitos, *Narrative Structure* 173. Beaton's text presents some problems since he prints Lambert's text, but includes tacit corrections of hers in the translation. Moreover, he has omitted in his translation S 1926, which as he prints it makes no sense at all. Finally, S 1925 should be translated as 'Call for the innmistress, not, stranger, for the innmaster' and not 'Call her a woman-innkeeper, not, stranger, an innkeeper', the omitted verse being 'since an innmistress can never be an innmaster', i.e. a woman cannot be a man.

[202] See Gregor von Nazianz, *De vita sua*: Einleitung, Text, Übersetzung, Kommentar. Herausgegeben, eingeleitet und erklärt von Ch. Jungck [Wissenschaftliche Kommentare zu griechischen und lateinischen Schriftstellern] (Heidelberg 1974).

[203] Note in particular 162-163 πάντων δὲ κοινὸν θάνατον δεδοικότων / ὁ κρυπτὸς ἦν ἔμοιγε φρικωδέστερος.

[204] 1919 πάρειμι νεκρὸς ἔμπνοος. The motif of death is at the same time combined with the motif of the road, since Gregorios - although dead - wins the 'athletic' contest of his road to God (1920-1922, 1945-1949).

romances can be explained on the common ground of basic beliefs and education, valid for all Byzantine cultural products.

In this sense the false death of the romance character is not as easily compatible between the various works. First, in the Palaiologian works it is only the hero who might undergo a false death. Second, while only in *Belthandros* do we find a false death scene over an actual corpse, both in *Kallimachos* and in *Livistros* the protagonists 'die' by magic means from the hands of a witch and are rescued by the very instrument of their death (an apple and a ring respectively). There is not a single comparable scene in the three Komnenian texts, where the characters are only supposed dead without an actual corpse present. This again contrasts with the ancient novels, where the misunderstandings take place over the supposed or real corpses (supposed corpses in Chariton and Tatios, real corpses in Tatios and Heliodoros). Viewed in this light the similarities between the *Digenis* and the *Achilleid*, which Beaton sees, become tenuous. Moreover, Beaton is willing to withdraw his early date of the *Achilleid* in order to accept the influence on the text by *Livistros*. Where then is the 'rigorously historical method'?

The analysis of specific scenes and motifs in three out of the five 'original' romances (it remains unclear why Beaton omits the *Achilleid* and the *Byzantine Iliad* from his analysis) moves along the lines already discussed. It is too simplistic an approach to suggest that similarity of names or of their sounds presupposes knowledge or even reference to the ancient novels. The use of 'ancient' names in the *Kallimachos* is but one of the necessary distancing devices in a work of fiction. This is not different from the use of names in dialogues, as in the case of the anonymous *Timarion* or Nikephoros Gregoras' *Phlorentios*: it is part of the genre's fictionality. But it is pulled by the hair that the name 'Kallimachos' alludes to the Hellenistic poet (147).

Beaton's attempt to explain the image of Chrysorrhoe hanging by her hair from the vaulted ceiling of the Giant's bedroom as consisting of a projection of the meaning 'to be in a state of erotic suspense or desire' of the verb κρεμῶμαι and the image of the girl leaning out of her window (*Dros.* iv 412 where κρεμωμένην is used) is improbable. And it is improbable because it presupposes a series of imagery shifts very hard to explain for medieval authors. Such a scene must be understood as looking back to a coherent image, that of the 'dangling virgin' for example: there is Andromeda from the mythological stock, St.Catherine or St.Barbara from hagiography, as well as various fictional instances - just to use some comparative material - in the *Thousand and One Nights*. For what is important here is the idea of 'beauty in distress', a crucial *topos* in erotic literature as devised by male authors. That such an image may include undertones of male *Angst* towards female sexuality is also possible.²⁰⁵ But not in the way Beaton explains the nature of the Giant as an anti-Eros, which supposedly is developed from an image in Eugenianos. In *Dros.* ii 216-219 δρακοντώδης γόνος means 'serpentlike creature' or 'offspring of serpents' and obviously refers to the peculiar nature of Eros as a destructive force. One should note that Eros was believed to have been born from an egg, a further connective element with his serpent-like nature.²⁰⁶ Even the bath scene in *Kallimachos* is not 'surely inspired' (149) from the βαλανεῖον dream in *Hysm.* v 1, since there are a number of things involved here.²⁰⁷

It would be tedious to enumerate and criticize all points in this section. Suffice it to say that Beaton (149) actually suggests that the river with the fiery star in *Belthandros* is an image developed from one specific line in Eugenianos (*Dros.* ii 382 ὦ πῦρ δροσίζον, ὦ φλογίζουσα δρόσος) which shows how far one can go in pressing 'genealogical' theories too much. We will omit further discussion and proceed to the second section of Chapter 10 with the title 'East meets West' (151-159).

Here Beaton embarks on an analysis of the Western elements found in the 'original' romances (the 'translated' ones are once again omitted since they *a priori* prove that Western literature was known to Byzantine authors). On the basis of generalizing statements ('It seems probable that most if not all of the translations were made in western-held lands' [151]) Beaton suggests that 'one would therefore expect that Constantinopolitan writers would be aware of developments in the western romance of the twelfth and thirteenth centuries; and we have already detected evidence that this was true even of Efstathios Makremvolitis' (*ibid.*). We have here a wonderful case of circular argumentation. The 'knowledge' of Western literature for Makrembolites is based on Carolina Cupane's study, '"Ερως βασιλεύς' (1974) and Beaton's own remarks in his

---

[205] On the question of the 'dangling virgin' motif and its sexual aspects see Eva Cantarella, 'Dangling virgins: Myth, Ritual and the Place of Women in Ancient Greece', in: Susan Rubin Suleiman (ed.), *The Female Body in Western Culture. Contemporary Perspectives* (Cambridge, Mass.-London 1987) 57-67.

[206] Cf. RE vi col. 488 and Aristoph. *Aves* 695 for the idea that Eros is born from an egg.

[207] See Agapitos, ClMed 41 (1990) 271f. Moreover, in *Kallimachos* the two lovers consummate their love in the bath, they are not just involved in erotic foreplay (see *Kall.* 781-782 and the references of Chrysorrhoe to this very scene at 2457-68).

analysis of that romance (77-79), all of which are pulled by the hair.[208] There is in fact no evidence at all for Western influence in Makrembolites, especially in the case of the figure of Eros on which most of Cupane's arguments are based.[209] In this sense one should be careful not to build a theory on already shaky foundations. In trying to suggest that the authors of the 'original' romances were indeed original, Beaton proceeds to look at 'literary *topoi* and to show how Greek models have been subtly adapted to come closer to their western counterparts' (151), an approach pioneered - as Beaton rightly grants - by Carolina Cupane. What follows is a short list of allusions to Latins (152) and a broad discussion of the two *topoi* that Cupane researched, namely 'Eros the King' and 'the Castle'. We would like to ask: are there no other *topoi* than these two to support Cupane's hypothesis, and if there are, why did Beaton not point them out to us? This question remains unanswered.

Beaton himself remarks that 'the teasing out' (151) of allusions to Latins is not a particularly useful procedure. And Beck had justly remarked that all of the references to Westerners in the vernacular romances are superficial and traceable back to the 11th and 12th centuries, either as Western influence (words like λίζιος) or as actually Byzantine customs (falcon-hunting).[210] It is therefore completely out of place for Beaton to suggest that 'in such allusions the writers of the three romances, at least, were

---

[208] Beaton suggests that Hysmine comes from Ysmaine (the name of Antigone's sister Ismene in the *romans d'antiquité*) and that Ἀρτύκομις (a city of the Rhine, river of the Celts) [Hercher i 241, 18-19] is an allusion to the *roi Artu*, legendary king of the Celts; that is the reason for the ypsilon in the non-sensical name. We do not have to make any comments on this. Yet it should be pointed out that Makrembolites used a very elaborate system of words, syntax and massive allusions to ancient Greek authors, as they are not so present in Prodromos and Eugenianos. For us the spelling Ὑσμίνη and Ὑσμινίας is nothing else but an optic inversion of the conventional Ἰσμήνη and Ἰσμηνίας (both fully attested names in Greek literature and Byzantine lexicography), which were at any rate pronounced exactly the same way while 'Ysma*i*ne' was not. As far as Ἀρτύκομις goes, the root ἀρτυ- means quite a lot in Greek, if Beaton had only cared to look up the dictionaries. There he would have learned that in Hesychios, the rare word ἀρτύς means 'friendship, judgement, treaty' (cf. Hesych. A7539 [ed.Latte]), exactly the essence of the city at the end of the romance, where 'friendship' is established after the 'judgement' on Hysmine's virginity is pronounced. We are afraid that what Beaton does here is a wild-goose chase, which then ends up becoming a grand feast of facts.

[209] On the figure of Eros in Cupane's argumentation, see Agapitos, ClMed 41 (1990) 268 n. 48; on the imperial imagery of Eros see above p. 37.

[210] Beck, *Volksliteratur* 125-126; see also the broader analysis in chapter 6 of his *Byzantinisches Erotikon*. On falcon-hunting in pre-12th century Byzantium one should add some interesting evidence from art. See the enamel medaillons (11th cent.) affixed on the Pala d'Oro (K.Wessel, *Die byzantinische Emailkunst* [Recklinghausen 1967] no. 46v and pp. 151-152) and some preserved pieces of luxurious silk embroidery (Marielle Martiniani-Reber, 'Le thème du Cavalier Chasseur d'après deux soieries byzantines conservées aux musées de Liège et de Lyon', Byzantion 55 [1985] 258-266).

acknowledging their own respect for their western peers in the romance genre' (152). No such attitude can be extracted from the texts. What is interesting, however, concerning the five 'original' romances, is that each one of them has a world of its own with distinct shadings: the *Achilleid* and the *Byzantine Iliad* a 'Trojan' setting (more so in the latter than in the former), *Kallimachos* a fictional wonder-tale world, *Belthandros* the regions of Central Anatolia and the 'Roman' empire, *Livistros* finally the 'exotic' lands of Armenia, Egypt and an undetermined Latin kingdom (Libandros). It is in fact *Livistros* that has the highest percentage of Latin elements (Livistros and his country are Latins, Rhodamne is dressed in Western style, a lance jousting takes place) but at the same time includes also the highest percentage of Byzantine elements (the figure of Eros at its most Byzantine, full ceremonial procedures according to Byzantine protocol). How is one to interpret this? We prefer to see an attempt by the authors to create specific 'fictional' worlds of their choice, with a very contemporary flavour, yet at the same time remote, in order to allow fictionality to function. Since the use of the 'atticizing' language had necessitated a *de rigueur* 'ancient' setting, the absence of this constraint leaves a vacuum. One could suggest - although this is only a hypothesis - that the 'historical, exotic' world of *Livistros* is closest to the bourgeois milieu of the Komnenian novel, which also favours exotic but historically recognizable settings. The closeness of *Livistros* to certain aspects of Makrembolites' and Eugenianos' works may even further point to chronological proximity. Whereas the wonder-tale world of *Kallimachos* with its omnipresent 'folkloric' elements and its fascinating sexual character appears to us as a later stage in the fortunes of the romance in late Byzantium. One would be tempted to suggest a mid-to-late 13th century date for *Livistros* (i.e. within the context of the Nicean or early Palaiologian court) and an early 14th century one for *Kallimachos*. At any rate, there is a long way to go to reach such conclusions, since the absence of a detailed study of *all* stylistic, motivic and structural aspects of *all* romances leaves us without a basis for such chronological constructs.

But let us return to the *topoi* discussed by Beaton on the basis of Cupane's studies. Beaton accepts her proposal that there is a direct development in the figure of Eros from Makrembolites to *Livistros* via *Kallimachos* and *Belthandros*, considering that 'this line of dependence is demonstrated in detail and is absolutely persuasive' (152).[211] This is by itself not so simple. Cupane is intent on proving a dependancy based on the traditional chronology, therefore being a dependancy of accretion. But the evidence could be turned

---

[211] Carolina Cupane,' Ἔρως βασιλεύς. La figura di Eros nel romanzo d'amore', in: Atti dell Academia di scienze, lettere e arti di Palermo, Ser. iv 33. 2. 2 (1974) 243-297.

the other way around: Makrembolites' highly complex and extended imagery is paralleled by *Livistros* followed - if one wants to use these categories - by *Belthandros* and finally by *Kallimachos* in a process of decretion and abstraction. However, we agree with Beaton who rightly criticizes Cupane's hypothesis of the Western origins of Makrembolites' imagery that does not function neither in terms of reception and development nor of chronology.[212]

Beaton concentrates on the figure of Eros in *Livistros*. Cupane had argued that the Western figure of the *Dieu d'Amour* has here fully taken over, pushing the boy-archer aside. Both Beaton and Cupane attempt to explain the actual appearance of "Ἔρως τριμορφοπρόσωπος. But a reading of the various passages in question (*Liv.* **N** 293-304, 513-519, 528, 531, 711-714 + **P** 577-584 [= **E** 849-857] + **N** 725-729) makes obvious that a syncretistic interpretation is impossible: the appearance of Eros remains vague. In fact, the god seems to appear under different guises in various situations (the authoritarian ruler in his first appearance, as the boy-archer in Livistros' second dream, as the flying cupid in Livistros' third dream [**N** 693-698] and Rhodamne's dream [**S** 196-211]). Similarly, Livistros' explanations on the nature of Eros (**N** 711-729), which are in reality the sibyllinic pronouncements of the Prophet in the 'room of oaths', cannot be brought to a coherent picture (besides the fact that the text is in a bad condition). Beaton suggests that the style of Klitovon's question and still more of Livistros' answer, is reminiscent of theological discussions of the nature of the Trinity (155). For this hypothesis he adduces no evidence. And indeed, there is no evidence to support such a suggestion, for the fact that we have three facets of a god does not suffice to imply trinitarian dogmatics, much less actual reminiscences of theological discussions. One thing is certain, that the middle face of Eros is not a 'grown youth in the prime of life' and it does not correlate to Makrembolites' μειράκιον, which is a beardless teenager. The *Livistros*-author describes it as 'τὸ δεύτερον ἐφαίνετον ὡς μέσης ἡλικίας / νὰ ἔχῃ τὸ γένιν στρογγυλόν, τὴν ὄψιν ὡς τὸ χιόνι' (**N** 298-299). These are not the attributes of a grown youth, but of a comely man in his middle years. In fact, the combination of a round beard with a snow-like skin is a characteristic trait of a

---

[212] Beaton, however, misses Cupane's point when he presents Eros sitting on a chariot, because this is exactly what Cupane does not want. Eros, according to her, sits on a throne. As Agapitos, ClMed 41 (1990) 270 n. 54 has argued, the expression Κροίσου δίφρος (*Hysm.* ii 7, 1-2) means 'Lydian chariot' and not 'the throne of Kroisos'. We would like also to point out that the description of Eros with wings all around his body is not so absurd, as Beaton thinks (153), but clearly reflects the traditional iconography of the angelic hosts, the six-winged cherubim and seraphim.

middle Byzantine emperor in his ideal beauty.[213] One should therefore be cautious in postulating development theories before all the evidence has been properly studied and discussed.

The chapter concludes with the second *topos* of Western-Eastern contact developed by Cupane, that of the Castle.[214] Beaton wholeheartedly accepts her arguments based on the same chronological scheme as she had used for the figure of Eros, that the appearance of the castle is a Western motif, which develops from a concrete (*Digenis*) to an allegorical (Meliteniotes) presentation. More recently Cupane developed also the structural position of the castle in the narrative, which - according to her - also reflects Western techniques (division between an *avanture* and an *amour* section of the texts).[215] Cupane's hypothesis is very attractive and at first sight fully convincing. Yet, there are a number of points which do not allow the drawing of such a neatly coherent picture. For one thing, and Beaton points it out without drawing any appropriate conclusions, the castle description appears in both the **E** and **G** version of the *Digenis*, both of which antedate the French *chateau d' amour*. But more important, not all castles in the various romances are the same. In fact, in some cases they are not even castles.[216] The basic misconception lies in the nature of the word κάστρον itself, which in the Byzantine sources means 'castle' but also '(walled) town'. It is most important to understand that the concept of the late antique (and early Byzantine) town with its open spaces, absence of fortifications etc. had

---

[213] See the description of Konstantinos ix Monomachos in Psellos' *Chronographia* vi 125-126 (Impellizeri ii 66-70).

[214] Carolina Cupane, 'Il motivo del castello nella narrativa tardobizantina. Evoluzione di un' allegoria', JÖB 27 (1978) 229-267.

[215] 'Topica romanzesca in oriente e in occidente: 'avanture' e 'amour'', in: H.-G. Beck - F. Conca - Carolina Cupane, *Il romanzo tra cultura latina e bizantina*. Testi della III settimana residenziale di studi medievali (Carini, Villa Belvedere 17-21 Ottobre 1983, a cura di C. Roccaro [Biblioteca dell' Encheiridion 5] (Palermo 1986) 47-72. In yet another article Cupane has taken up Beck's study *Byzantinisches Erotikon* (cf. above n. 32) on the question of the romances, formulating in a concise way her general views on the whole question ('Byzantinisches Erotikon: Ansichten und Einsichten', JÖB 37 [1987] 213-233).

[216] For a particularly absurd case see Beaton 156 on *Ach*. **N** 843-878 where Achilles' painting of Eros is classified along with passages from the *Kallimachos* exemplifying Eros' connections with castles. No castle is mentioned here.

radically changed in the middle Byzantine period.[217] The middle Byzantine town is a small fortified citadel, often placed around the *akropolis* of the late antique city, its walls filled with debris from the ruins.[218] A quick glance at the romances suggests that some of the *kastra* belong to this very type of medieval town. Most prominent among these is *Argyrokastron* in *Livistros*, which appears as a triangular fortress or a walled town, according to the specific situation. Similarly the *Drakontokastron* in *Kallimachos* is often referred to as πόλις.[219] We must therefore assume a 'fluid' concept of these *kastra*, where the authors use one or the other or both meanings together in order to highlight the given scene.

In one major instance the supposed castle is not present at all. This is the 'Erotokastron' in *Livistros*. Only too hastily did Cupane equate the *Erotokastron* in *Belthandros* with the similar scene in *Livistros*, an obvious mistake in her attempt to see a developmental line from the concrete to the allegorical. But the fact is that, while in *Belthandros* the place where Belthandros enters and where Eros appears to him is explicitly referred to as *Erotokastron* (*Belth.* 281, 327, 432, 441 etc.), the place where Livistros is brought to and where he meets Eros is never referred to as a *kastron* but as a *katouna* (**N** 269 and *passim*). It makes a big difference - granted that one takes the authors of these romances seriously - if an author uses *kastron* or *katouna*, especially in *Livistros* where the reader is later on confronted with a *kastron* called explicitly *Argyrokastron*, paralleling the *Drakontokastron* and *Erotokastron* of *Kallimachos* and *Belthandros* respectively. Moreover, a comparison between the structural elements of Eros' *katouna* and *Argyrokastron* shows that there are no repetitions of buildings in the two spaces except for a pool with a *phiale* topped by a statue.[220] It has been argued elsewhere[221] that the *katouna* is the military camp of the Byzantine emperor transferred

---

[217] On this question see E. Kirsten, *Die byzantinische Stadt* [Berichte zum XI Internationalen Byzantinistenkongress, V.3] (München 1958) and D. Claude, *Die byzantinische Stadt im 6.Jahrhundert* [Byzantinisches Archiv 13] (München 1969). For a more recent synoptic synthesis with further bibliography see C. Foss - D. Winfield, *Byzantine Fortifications. An Introduction* (Pretoria 1986) 7-13 and H. Saradi-Mendelovici, 'The Demise of the Ancient City and the Emergence of the Medieval City in the Eastern Roman Empire', Classical Views n. s. 7 (1988) 365-401. For the lexicographical material on κάστρον as 'walled/fortified town' see Kriaras, Λεξικό s.v. 2.

[218] A good example is Sardis, for which see C. Foss, *Byzantine and Turkish Sardis* (Cambridge, Mass. 1976).

[219] For detailed references in *Livistros* and *Kallimachos* see Agapitos, ClMed 41 (1990) n. 30.

[220] For the possible meaning of the two fountains with the two statues, see Agapitos, *Narrative Structure* 329.

[221] Agapitos, *Narrative Structure* 189-190, 305-314 (*Argyrokastron*) and 323-327 (Eros' *katouna*).

to the fantastic world of dreams and the domain of Emperor Eros. In this sense, the figure of Eros is far more Byzantine than has so far been admitted.

Finally, it has been argued - persuasively in our opinion - that the garden as 'space characterizing female sexuality' which makes its first appearance in the ancient works and is fully used in the Komnenian texts, is fused with the castle in representing the 'fortified space' in which the female protagonist remains.[222] Beaton accepts this and further suggests that we have here a metaphorical shading deriving from a long tradition (158-159 with quotations from Basilakes and Makrembolites). Well, in this case, we would argue, the notion of the fortified place - be it enclosed garden, castle or town - can be explained within Graecobyzantine tradition without the Western model of the *chateau d'amour* which develops from its own roots in Latin poetry and medieval tradition.

We shall conclude this chapter with Beaton's discussion of *Argyrokastron* in *Livistros*. Beaton explains the triangular form of the castle as the author's desire to incorporate the same elements as were present in Makrembolites' depiction of Eros, but more than that as a symbolic parallelism between the triadic nature of Eros himself and the three sides of the fortress. Be that as it may, Beaton proceeds to interpret the castle as a physical extension of Rhodamne herself in symbolical terms (157). This he supports by a number of passages, the first being the advice of the Friend to Livistros to write letters and shoot them into Rhodamne's chambers (S 61-68). It is worthwhile to concentrate for a moment on this passage, because it shows how dangerous it can be to interpret a text without having a clear picture of the textual problems involved. This is Beaton's text (except for our restoration of the traditional breathings and accents):

γράψε εἰς σαγίτταν γράμματα· ὅταν ἴδῃς ἀπέκει
ἀπὸ τὸ πανεξαίρετον τῆς κόρης τὸ κουβοῦκλι
ὅτι προκύπτει (ἡ) ἐρωτικὴ κἂν μία τὸ νὰ μᾶς βλέψῃ,
[ποῖσε ἀφορμὴν ὅτι θεωρεῖς πουλὶν εἰς τὸ κουβοῦκλιν, E 1192]
καὶ τόξευσέ το ἀχαμνὰ καὶ πρόσεξε νὰ πέσῃ
ἀπέσω εἰς τὸ κουβοῦκλιν της τῆς κόρης ἡ σαγίττα,
καὶ τέως νὰ δώσῃς ἀφορμὴν καὶ ἀρχὴν εἰς τὴν ἀγάπην,
καὶ νὰ ἴδῃς τὸ ἐπιχείρημα τὸ πῶς νὰ τὸ ἐμπέσῃ.

It does not become clear from any footnote how the passage is to be read. The obvious inference of the reader is that the verse in angular brackets with the reference 'E 1192'

---

[222] Littlewood, *op. cit.* (above n. 40).

fills a gap in the **S** version.[223] The article ἡ in parentheses (**S** 63) must represent Beaton's own addition, as can be inferred from its inclusion in his translation ('the loved one'). The passage is then interpreted sexually: the arrow of Livistros 'enters' Rhodamne's bedchamber (just like Eros' arrow had entered Rhodamne's heart), while the words πουλίν (**E** 1192) and ἀχαμνά (**S** 65) are intensifying the sexual context. Beaton (231 n. 19) refers to the Modern Greek meaning of πουλίν as 'penis' and ἀχαμνά as 'testicles'. We fail, however, to see how these anachronistic meanings can be made to fit this context: whose πουλίν is to be shot and to whose ἀχαμνά? Clearly, πουλί and ἀχαμνά are used without any sexual colouring in the text, the one as an excuse for Livistros to shoot an arrow (the πουλίν therefore is to be assumed close to Rhodamne's quarters), the other as the spatial adverb within Rhodamne's balcony. One should be careful with these things!

But to return to the actual text of the romance. In fact, **S** does not have a lacuna but transmits as **S** 63-64 ἕνα προκύψει ἡ ἐρωτικὴ κἂν μία τὸ νὰ μᾶς βλέψῃ / ποίησε ἀπέδω ἀφορμὴν ὅτι θεωρεῖς τὸ κουβοῦκλιν. The remaining versions look as follows: **N** 1040-1041 ὅτι προσκύψει ἐρωτικὴ καμμία τοῦ νὰ μᾶς βλέπῃ / ποῖσε ἀφορμὴν ὅτι θεωρεῖς πουλὶν εἰς τὸ κουβοῦκλιν : **P** and **Σ**[224] omit the lines: **E** ὅτι προσκύπτει ἡ ἐρωτικὴ καμμία της νὰ μᾶς βλέπῃ / ποῖσε ἀφορμὴν ὅτι θεωρεῖς πουλὶν εἰς τὸ κουβοῦκλιν (Lambert). It is instructive to give for the sake of comparison the unpublished text of **V** f. 42v-43r, so that the reader may form an idea of the differences involved (spelling and accentuation have been normalized):

γράψε εἰς σαΐτταν γράμματα καὶ γόμο τὸ δοξάριν·[225]
καὶ ὅταν ἰδῇς τὰς βάϊες τῆς κόρης // [f.43v] τῆς Ροδάμνης
ποῖσε ἀφορμὴ πουλὶ βλέπεις ἀπάνω εἰς τὸ κουβοῦκλιν·[226]
καὶ σύρνεις τάχα εἰς τὸ πουλίν, καὶ ἐσὺ ρίξε
εἰς τῆς κόρης τὸν ἡλιακὸν καὶ εἰς τὸ παραθῦριν·[227]

---

[223] The reader bases this on Beaton's own remark (103) - for which see our comments above p. 59 - that where gaps appear on the right hand page of Lambert's edition one crosses over to the left-hand page (i.e. from the **S** to the **E** version).

[224] **Σ** (or **S1** according to Lambert) is the fragment transmitting the disordered sequence **S** 1433-1513 + **P** 1125-1393) for which see Agapitos, *Narrative Structure* 28.

[225] The form γόμο is the imperative of the verb γομῶ/γομώνω ('to fill'); the more common form of the present tense simple aspect imperative would be γόμωσε.

[226] Interestingly enough the MS transmits πουλή βλεπεις, in which case the lack of accent on the verb could indicate that it is conceived as an enclitic to the oxytonal noun.

[227] These two verses are like prose, a fairly common occurence in **V**, similar to the London *Achilleid* and the *Belthandros*.

Καὶ τόξευσε ἐπιτήδεια νὰ πέσῃ εἰς τὸν τόπον,
τέως νὰ δώσῃς ἀφορμήν, ἀρχὴν εἰς τὴν ἀγάπην,
νὰ ἰδῇς τὸ ἐπιχείρημα, τὸ τί ἀρχὴ νὰ ἔχῃ.

First of all, the article ἡ in **S** 63 is very much present in the manuscript. Moreover, Beaton's version of the first half-verse in **S** 63 completely distorts what is in the manuscript, since ὅτι is taken over from **E** 1191 and the verb appears as προκύπτει, which is an arbitrary combination of **S**'s προκύψει and **E**'s προσκύπτει. But the meaning of **S** is clear if the spelling is normalized correctly. In **S** 63 ἕνα does not mean 'one', but ἵνα (a typical phonetic change like εἶναι > ἔναι); thus προκύψει must be normalized to προκύψῃ, making the tenses of the passage coherent in their simple aspect (προκύψῃ - βλέψῃ - ποίησε etc.). **S** 64 makes good sense ('make from now on an excuse that you are looking at the chamber'), even if the specific excuse of the bird is lacking and the verse has one extra syllable in its second half. The presence of the bird in versions **NEV** and its absence in **P** and **Σ** shows that one should not add the one or the other verse, substituting it for something else. Versions **NEV** have to be seen on their own accord.

The other passage which Beaton adduces to support his suggestion that the castle is a physical extension of Rhodamne comes from one of Livistros' letters to her. Beaton does not quote the whole letter (**S** 278-299), but only the lines **S** 285-287 and 295-296. But even these five lines make clear that the castle referred to is Livistros' heart (cf. **S** 278-279 Πότε νὰ ἐπεριεπάτησες τὸ κάστρον τῆς ψυχῆς μου, / πότε τὸν πύργον τῆς ἐμῆς καρδίας νὰ ἐδιέβης;), not Rhodamne's. It is Rhodamne who appears as the destructive force, the ἑλέπολις of the male bastion. This is a conventional inversion of the '*militat omnis amans*' image.[228] This passage therefore cannot be brought in as proof for Beaton's hypothesis. It is much more convenient and plausible to see *Argyrokastron* as the obstacle (see, e.g., **S** 439) which has to be overcome and which only Livistros succeeds in doing.

Enough, we think, has been said on this issue. What emerges is that superficial analysis for the supposed 'genealogical' affiliations of the romances will not do. We have complex intertextual procedures before us which need to be explained in successive stages: these are, of course, linked with each other, but they must be separated and studied carefully, be it textual, metrical, linguistic or literary problems, before synthetic conclusions can be reached. The analysis of the two *topoi* Eros and Castle demonstrated that

---

[228] On this inversion see Marcelle Thiébaux, *The Stag of Love. The Chase in Medieval Literature* (Ithaca, N. Y. 1974).

it is not enough to base one's research on previous studies, unless their results have been thoroughly checked. Beaton's conclusion of Chapter 10 (159) goes to show that he wavers between the lack of evidence and the accepted results of Cupane's studies.

Chapter 11

Common elements of the romances:
oral background vs textual interference

In this chapter Beaton discusses the three main theories that have been brought forward to account for the verbal similarities in the texts and the differences between the manuscript witnesses for those texts that have been transmitted in more than one manuscript. The outcome of his analysis is that he accepts something from each of them, in order to construe his own explanation which is basically the idea of the author/copyist working consciously in a new medium to create a fictional tradition.

The three theories discussed are the following: 1) the oral-formulaic theory associated with the names of Michael and Elizabeth Jeffreys; 2) Giuseppe Spadaro's theory of literary borrowings; and 3) Arnold Van Gemert and Wim Bakker's theory of scribal interference.

We have no objection to the way in which Beaton presents these theories (161-164); he is very fair to all of them, also on points where he disagrees. Then follows a section in which he offers critique of the theories. He starts with a discussion of scribal interference. Now, as is well known, Bakker and Van Gemert have built their theory on the Naples manuscript iii. B. 27 (**N**) which contains the *Achilleid*, the *Belisarios* and the *Imberios* written by the same scribe throughout.[229] According to their view the scribe(s) of the Naples MS copied these texts from an exemplar which had these same texts, and in which (or in the immediate ancestor) the scribe coming from copying the *Achilleid* would interfere with the following texts, the *Belisarios* and the *Imberios*. In this way Bakker and Van Gemert would account for the verbal similarities between these texts (they also include the *Florios*, but it is not easy to see how it relates to **N**) and would also explain how the differences between the various manuscripts of the same text are generated. Beaton agrees in principle; he claims that

> 'when the same text is preserved in more than one manuscript there is not a single case in the whole of medieval Greek vernacular literature of a text being reproduced exactly. The variations which are almost always at the level

---

[229] An analysis of the various hands and sections of this MS can be found in D.Michailidis, Rivista di studi bizantini e neoellenici 8-9 (1971-1972) 272 (cf. above n. 123).

of wording rather than of changes to the story, are clearly due to the copyists.' (165)

Firstly, it should be pointed out that there are in fact examples of exact reproduction, as we have mentioned above p. 52. Secondly, there is a *petitio principii* here. For what does Beaton mean by saying 'the same text'? We would argue that it has to be proven that we have to do with the same text, or, in other words that the manuscripts are descended from the same *archetypus*. In the case of the *Digenis*, for example, we do not regard it as proven that there once was an original *Digenis* from which the extant manuscripts (or versions, as we would prefer) are descended in such a way that a stemma can meaningfully be construed. Nor in the cases of the *Achilleid* and *Livistros* does it make much sense to attempt making up a stemma in order to reconstruct a lost original. And thirdly, the point about the responsibility of the scribes has to be stated more precisely. We agree, of course, that scribes make mistakes of every imaginable sort. They do so irrespective of whether they copy Plato or the *Achilleid*. We also agree that scribes may change the text they are copying, if they encounter difficulties, if they cannot read their *Vorlage*, if they grow sleepy, or think of something other than the work they have in hand etc. But we cannot see why we should have to accept that scribes change the texts they are copying without any such reason. The great problem in Beaton's image of medieval Greek scribes is that he does not acknowledge that these men were professional artisans, that they were conscientious about their work and tried to execute it as best they could. They were certainly not would-be poets. At least the *onus probandi* lies entirely with those who hold them to be doing the opposite of what they are being paid to do: namely to prepare a copy of their *Vorlage*.[230] The only case we can think of in Byzantine vernacular poetry, where we can see a scribe doing what Beaton, Bakker and Van Gemert suspect they all did, is sufficiently special so as not to be the rule. Demetrios Zinos who was responsible for the philological editing of the *Theseid* when it was prepared as a chapbook for a Venetian press probably in 1528, can be seen at work in his autograph manuscript, *Vat. Pal. gr.* 426 where he without much consideration for the text of Boccaccio makes extensive changes in his own manuscript, which may have been copied from *Par. gr.* 2898 with an edition in mind; as suggested above p. 71, one might

---

[230] The first chapter in Alphonse Dain's authoritative *Les Manuscrits* (3e ed. Paris 1975) gives a convincing and sympathetic portrait of the scribe and his work. This should be required reading for any scholar who ventures an opinion about scribal procedure. We would like to quote p. 40: 'Voilà donc analysé le travail du copiste et de ses aides, technique qui relève à la fois de la science et de l' art. Souvent nos gens avaient le sentiment qu'ils travaillaient pour l'humanité, et je gage que plus d'un copiste a soupçonné que son modeste labeur était pour lui un moyen de laisser son nom à la posterité. Mais d'aucuns, j'en suis sûr, n'ont eu d'autre satisfaction, avec leur médiocre salaire, que la conscience d'un travail bien fait.'

account for the differences between the two manuscripts on the theory that Zinos already from the start had the printing exemplar in mind.[231] Anyway, this is a wholly different situation, and one not likely to pertain to the manuscripts of the other romances. We also point to the fact that Zinos is rather a scholar than a scribe. His efforts in the Vatican MS may be paralleled with what we know of other Byzantine scholars and their working exemplars.[232]

The lack of information about the scribes who wrote our vernacular texts is a serious drawback. Not a single one has been identified by name (except for Zinos), and we do not know anything about the scribe Demetrios who subscribed on f. 78v in the famous Vienna *theol. gr.* 244 (**V**).[233] There is no doubt, however, that this man was a professional

---

[231] On this see E. Follieri, 'La versione in greco volgare del Teseida del Boccaccio', *Atti dell' viii Congresso internazionale di studi bizantini* (Roma 1953) 67-77 (when it had not yet been realized that Zinos was the scribe of the Vatican MS, cf. n. 176) and Birgit Olsen, ClMed 41 (1990) 277-278.

[232] See e.g. the MS used as 'Druckvorlage' for Musuros' Aristophanes (1498), *Selest.* 347 written by Zacharias Kalliergis, a page of which has been reproduced in *Griechische Handschriften und Aldinen. Eine Ausstellung anlässlich der XV. Tagung der Mommsen-Gesellschaft in der Herzog August Bibliothek Wolfenbüttel* (Herzog August Bibliothek Wolfenbüttel Mai 1978) pl. 50b; also the page from the Sophocles MS, Leningrad 741 (*op. cit.* pl. 52), used for Ioannes Gregoropoulos' 1502 edition (usually ascribed to Musuros, but see Martin Sicherl's comments accompanying the plate). Further, one may compare the extensive additions and corrections to the *Rhetorica ad Alexandrum* in *Par. gr.* 2038 (a page reproduced in M. Fuhrmann, *Untersuchungen zur Textgeschichte der pseudo-aristotelischen Alexander-Rhetorik* [Akademie der Wissenschaften und der Literatur in Mainz. Abhandlungen der Geistes- und sozialwissenschaftlichen Klasse Jahrgang 1964, Nr. 7] [Wiesbaden 1965] Abb.1). This MS served as printer's copy for the Aldine edition 1509 (see Ole L. Smith, ClMed 37 [1986] 258 n. 9 and references to Sicherl's findings *ibid.*); it was not written by Andronikos Kallistos, but by the hand Smith has proposed to label *Anonymus Mutinensis*, cf. ClMed 33 (1981-1982) 256-258. It would be interesting to be certain of the identity of this very prolific and scholarly scribe. In the new standard work on Greek scribes Harlfinger and Gamillscheg still accept the identification with Andronikos Kallistos, see *Repertorium* (full details above n. 176) 1. A. 18, 2. A. 25. See also now on the controversy Judy K. Deuling - John Cirignano, 'The Later ABS Family Manuscripts of Xenophon's *Hiero* Tradition', Scriptorium 44 (1990) 58 n. 29.

[233] It has often been asserted that the whole of **V** (cf. n. 167) has been written by the same scribe throughout. This is definitely not true, and we cannot help wondering how many of the scholars that have pronounced this verdict ever saw the whole of **V**. At least some did, including Hugo Schreiner who in his paper 'Die zeitliche Aufeinanderfolge der im Cod. Vindob. Theol. gr. 244 überlieferten Texte des Imberios, des Belisar und des Florios, und ihr Schreiber', BZ 55 (1962) 213-223 does not doubt for a moment that Demetrios was the scribe of the *Belisarios*-part also. The part containing the *Belisarios* ff. 227r-245r (and only this part) has been written by a wholly different hand (as was seen already by Sathas, cf. Wagner, *Carmina graeca medii aevi* XIII), and Bakker-Van Gemert's confident statement 'γραμμένο ἀπὸ τὸ ἴδιο χέρι' (their *Belisarios* edition p. 48) is either mistaken or proof that they never saw anything other than the *Belisarios* part. Isavella Tsavari in her edition of the *Poulologos* p. 47 is more careful and does not commit herself. She says that the greater part of the manuscript is written by Demetrios.

scribe, not an amateur.[234] The same goes for the scribes of the Naples codex iii. B. 27 (**N**) and for that matter, also for the scribe of the somewhat earlier Escorial manuscript (Ψ. iv. 22) containing *Digenis* and *Livistros*.

There is no need, and we still have got to see evidence in that direction, to assume *a priori* that the professional scribes treat their *Vorlage* more cavalierly when they are copying vernacular texts than they do when copying other texts. Thus it will not do to put the blame on the scribes. No doubt they had difficulties with the orthography and the morphology, trained as they were in the learned language without any codification of the vernacular to help.[235] Variations at this level are inescapable. All this seems to go back to H.-G. Beck,[236] but no evidence is given, no arguments adduced. It seems to be accepted as a *fable convenue*: since the texts must go back to a common exemplar, it must be the scribes who change the texts so much that the common exemplar disappears from sight and is impossible to reconstruct.[237]

The second point made by Bakker and Van Gemert and supported by Beaton is the following:

'that when more than one text is preserved *in the same manuscript* we find common elements throughout the manuscript, at the level of verbal expressions, which may not correspond with other manuscript versions of the same poems.' (165)

Beaton agrees with this and says that 'the intervention of copyists is ... not in doubt' (*ibid.*) referring to the Naples (iii. B. 27) and the Escorial (Ψ. iv. 22)

---

[234] According to Schreiner in the paper quoted in the preceding note Demetrios also wrote some liturgical MSS now in Moscow (*op.cit.* 214 n. 2). If this is correct we could be almost certain of his status as a regular professional copyist. We should add here the case of Nikolaos Sophianos who has been identified as the scribe of the MS containing the Tocco Chronicle (*Vat. gr.* 2214 [on which cf. Salvatore Lilla, *Codices Vaticani Graeci, codd. 2162-2254* (In Bibliotheca Vaticana 1985) 197]; see G. Schirò, Revue des études sud-est européennes 7 (1969) 209-219 (especially p. 210). Again in this case, the scribe is rather a scholar than an artisan.

[235] It is true that at least some of the vernacular MSS look as if they may not have been written by professional scribes, for instance parts of the Oxford MS of the *Achilleid* look very little professional. But the greater part of the MSS were certainly written by schooled copyists. This may be due to the character of most of these MSS: they were cleanly and professionally written products destined for the trade.

[236] In H. Hunger, *Geschichte der Textüberlieferung* Bd. I, 470ff (especially 480 and 483).

[237] The Jeffreys suggest that the scribes may have been working by reading a few lines and then writing them out, 'using the same mixture of memory and re-creation as the oral poets - an oral variant, if you wish, of the theory of "inner dictation"' (*Okeanos* 318). We cannot see why there is any need to mix orality into this; the scribes used the method also in copying out the learned texts, whereby all sorts of memories of similar phrases crept into the texts without necessarily compelling us to suppose that the scribes did so because they allowed themselves to be overtaken by poetical inspiration.

manuscripts. These two manuscripts are in our opinion neither proof of the theory, nor parallel cases. Now that Bakker and Van Gemert's edition of the *Belisarios* has appeared (it seems not to have been published when Beaton finished his book) it should be possible to judge their case on a better basis than their 1981 paper in Ελληνικά.[238]

The difficulties are several. First of all we have to assume that the *Achilleid*, the *Belisarios* and the *Imberios* have been transmitted together in two stages before the Naples MS was written around 1460. This is of course not impossible. Then we also have the problem that on this theory we should expect influence, on account of the order of the texts in the MS, from the *Achilleid* on the *Belisarios* and the *Imberios*, not the other way round. However, in the prolegomena to the *Belisarios* edition p. 76 n. 15 Bakker and Van Gemert imply that the movement has also gone the other way at least between the *Achilleid*, the *Imberios* and the *Florios*.

The greatest problems in this theory are, however, that it is not explained, why the scribes should act in this way. There is no rationale in their behaviour. They are not faced with difficulties in their exemplar, they are not improving the texts in any meaningful way. Then we also have to posit a number of intermediate stages in order to construe a stemma which we find highly unlikely and not really easy to explain historically. A glance at the complicated stemma for the *Belisarios* makes us doubt the validity of the theory.

Beaton is right, we think, in pointing out the danger of circular reasoning in the hunt for interpolations, and from his final summary of the scribal interference theory, we get the impression that he accepts it in the case of the *Belisarios* but does not think that it will account for the great mass of verbal similarities in the vernacular texts. As we shall see, in his own proposal he returns to the would-be poet/scribe who plays an important role in his own explanation.

It remains to be emphasized that the scribal interference has yet to be worked out for the Escorial manuscript. Until then we would think that the most obvious explanation of the particular make-up of this book is that the texts represent the personal selection

---

[238] 'Η Αχιλληίδα και η ιστορία του Βελισαρίου', Ελληνικά 33 (1981) 82-97.

of the scribe,[239] not a uniformity imposed on them by him.[240]

For good reasons, we think, Beaton is clearly more lukewarm towards Spadaro's theory, and it is not all unfair or untrue that Spadaro's ideas have been presented by the Jeffreys as a much more consistent whole than it really is. We cannot agree with Beaton that Spadaro's theory holds good even in the case of the *Achilleid* and the *Belisarios* (where, he says, a direct relationship has been confirmed) but there might be a case for *Imberios* having taken one line from *Florios*. Since Spadaro's case here has been accepted by the Jeffreys[241] and by Beaton (166), we have to take a closer look at it.

In the *Cantare di Fiorio e Biancifiore*[242] stanza 91 the lines

Quando l'avrai tu non porai morire

in fuoco, nè in aqua, nè in bataglia

have been translated thus in *Flor.* 1193-1195:

καὶ ὡς ὅτου νὰ ἔχῃς μετὰ σὲν τοῦτο τὸ δακτυλίδιν,

ποτὲ θανάτου συμφοράν, ποτὲ μηδὲν φοβᾶσαι,

οὐδὲ ἱστιάν, οὐδὲ νερόν, ἀλλ' οὐδὲ ἀπὸ ξίφος. [243]

There is indeed a strong presumption that the line 1195 in the Greek translation is a direct reflection of the Italian text. Now, according to Spadaro, when *Imberios* 230-233 has:

καὶ ὥστε τὸ ἐγκόλπιον βαστᾶς τὸ μετ' ἐσένα,

ποτὲ θανάτου συμφοράν, ποτὲ μηδὲν φοβᾶσαι,

οὐδὲ κοντάριν δύναται ποσῶς νὰ σὲ φονεύσῃ,

οὐδὲ ἱστία, οὐδὲ νερόν, ἀλλ' οὐδὲ ἀπὸ ξίφους

we would seem to have a good case of plagiarism. These are the texts as printed in Kriaras' edition. The Jeffreys, however with good reason reject the identical lines *Flor.*

---

[239] See Agapitos, *Narrative Structure* 30.

[240] Cf. also Jeffreys & Jeffreys, *Okeanos* 314 who correctly point out that the scribe's 'knowledge of the other texts involved is likely to have been gained in a preliminary reading rather than in the process of copying them', which is a situation similar to the one presumed by Spadaro's theory of plagiarism. One should note here that the *Par. gr.* 2909 (*Belthandros, Sachlikes, Belisarios* Λ and other texts) seems to constitute a similar case. Also in this MS there is a similarity in the linguistic level, and there are no rubrics. Cf. Agapitos, *Narrative Structure* 47 n. 38 and 96 n. 158.

[241] *Op.cit.* 320f. See Spadaro, Ἑλληνικά 28 (1975) 307ff.

[242] Quoted from *Il Cantare di Fiorio e Biancifiore* edito ed illustrato da Vincenzo Crescini vol.ii (Scelta di curiosità letterarie inedite o rare dal secolo xiii al xvii in appendice alla Collezione di opere inedite o rare. Dispensa ccii) (Bologna 1899) 168.

[243] This is Kriaras' text; for the MSS, see Spadaro, *loc. cit.* and Jeffreys & Jeffreys *loc. cit.* Besides, see also H. Schreiner, BZ 55 (1962) 215 with n. 12, who was the first to analyze this passage before Spadaro drew attention to it.

1194 = *Imb.* 231 as not being convincing proof of plagiarism by the author of the *Imberios*, but they accept *Flor.* 1195 = *Imb.* 233: 'This one line comes close to providing a formal proof of Spadaro's theory that the *Imberios* poet had plagiarised *Florios*.'

Now whatever really happened here, the Jeffreys and Beaton overlook two important points. One is that the crucial line *Imb.* 233, according to Kriaras' apparatus is omitted in two of the four manuscripts (**N**, Naples iii. B. 27 and **H**, *Vat. Pal. gr.* 426). The third manuscript **O**, Oxford *misc.* 287 puts the line after 234, which leaves us with **V**, Vienna *theol. gr.* 244 as the only witness to the *Imberios* with text and sequence of lines exactly as in the *Florios*. Could the misplacement of the line in **O** have something to do with its being a later interpolation in the *Imberios* text? Far from being an interpolation or an example of plagiarism by the author this case boils down to an individual initiative by the scribes of **O** and **V**. The second point that to our thinking suggests that Spadaro's case is not as clear-cut as it would seem from the Jeffreys' and Beaton is that the *Florios* text has been corrected by Kriaras from the *Imberios* in line 1194. The *Florios* MSS do not have ποτὲ μηδὲν φοβᾶσαι but ποτὲ μὴν ἀποθάνῃς (**V**) and υἱὲ νὰ μὴ ἀποθάνῃς (**L**), and there is no doubt that Kriaras corrected from the *Imberios* - where again only **V** has the text printed by Kriaras. As far as we can see there is some justification for not regarding the plagiarism by the author of *Imberios* as settled and beyond doubt. And if nothing else this case shows the dangers inherent in accepting Kriaras' text without looking into the apparatus.

A number of points in Beaton's discussion of Spadaro's work must be mentioned. He is sceptical about Spadaro's idea that the opening lines of the *War of Troy* served as model both for the **N** *Achilleid* (lines 20-28) and for the added proem to the *Theseid* (169). However, as far as the *Theseid* is concerned, Beaton follows Spadaro and thinks that the translator of the Italian text made a conscious allusion to another large-scale Greek translation of a foreign work. He deliberately chose this passage, and remodelled it to suit the *Theseid*. Beaton forgets, however, the point he makes himself on p. 172 that this manner of beginning was traditional in the Greek vernacular genre - which is the way in which he surely rightly explains the similar beginning of the *Achilleid* (from where Beaton in contrast to Spadaro believes that the translator of the *War of Troy* became inspired) and the typologically similar openings to the *Kallimachos*, *Belthandros* and the *Byzantine Iliad*.

There is one further point to be made in relation to the identical opening in the *Achilleid*, the *War of Troy* and the *Theseid* which illustrates what we said above about existing editions: the danger that they are regarded as standard texts. For what Beaton quotes here as *Achilleid* **N** 20 is Hesseling's correction:[244]

Εἷς τῶν Ἑλλήνων βασιλεύς, εὐγενικὸς καὶ ὡραῖος
πλούσιος καὶ πανευγενὴς ἐν χώρα Μυρμιδόνων

N has not εὐγενικός but πανευγενής in which case the identity between the first line in the three poems disappears. But Hesseling corrected the **N** *Achilleid* to make it conform with the *War of Troy*.[245] And there is no other reason why the text should be corrected. This can only make one wonder how many other cases of verbal identity have been introduced in other texts with (or without) a note in the apparatus (which no one reads). Further Beaton claims that the *Achilleid* narrative begins in two versions with these lines.[246] The London manuscript does not have the beginning at all in its present acephalous state, and **O**'s wording is different.[247] It is not clear which is the other version Beaton is thinking of. Later on the same page he speaks only about **N**.[248]

Finally, the Jeffreys' oral-formulaic point of view. The great problem here, of course, is that we have no evidence of an oral tradition in Byzantium behind the vernacular texts. On the other hand, it must be admitted that neither do we have any evidence of an oral tradition before the composition of the *Iliad* and the *Odyssey*. One of Milman Parry's great discoveries was that we had to assume a long tradition to account for the complex formulaic system in the Homeric poems. Now the Byzantine system is a far cry from the metrical and linguistic complexity which we find in Homeric formulas, but is rather similar to the South Slavic epic style.[249] Beaton rightly questions the hypothesis on which the Jeffreys have built their theory, but he admits on the other hand that there is a tradition to which the vernacular texts refer for authority. The repeated

---

[244] Spadaro, 'Sul Teseida Neogreco', Folia Neohellenica 2 (1977) 159 quotes the lines in the same form without any indication of what is the MS reading.

[245] Cf. Hesseling's edition of the **N** *Achilleid* p.14 and his commentary on l. 20.

[246] Spadaro *loc. cit.* says that the **O** text is a closer reflection of the *War of Troy* opening, but see next note.

[247] As for Beaton's speculations (170) about the translator having misunderstood line 20 in **N** ἐν χώρα Μυρμιδόνων (for which he according to Beaton gives a placename χώρας τῆς Μυρμιδόνος) it should be pointed out that the Oxford version treats μυρμυδόνα as a placename, as did the translator of the *Theseid*. This does certainly not prove dependence on the **N** text. And it should be pointed out that Spadaro, BZ 71 (1978) 4 n. 13 indicated that χώρας τῆς Μυρμιδόνος is the reading of MS *Coislin*. 344, whereas the other MS of the *War of Troy* containing this passage (*Bonon.* 3567) has χώρας δὲ Μυρμιδόνων. Which reading, then, is the original?

[248] There is also an error in the translation of the *Byz. Iliad* line 9 on p.171: εἶχεν ἡ Τροία ἔσωθεν does not mean 'he had inside Troy'.

[249] The differences between the Homeric oral poetry and the South Slav poems studied by Milman Parry and Albert Lord were summed up in G. S. Kirk's influential book *The Songs of Homer* (Cambridge 1962) 88-95. For a recent discussion of the controversy see John M. Foley, *The Theory of Oral Composition* (Bloomington & Indianapolis 1988) 61ff.

phrases, however, are not part of that tradition; they are, according to Beaton, the creation of the poets.

Beaton's own attempt is to make a synthesis. The shared elements, he says (178) are the effects of two causes: one is the consciously felt need to create a tradition of literary fiction in the vernacular; the other, that since the poets wrote in a medium connected with oral tradition they incorporated elements of plot and diction from the oral tradition, and tended like oral poets to repeat ready-made phrases.

The would-be poet-scribe makes at this point a reappearance in only slight disguise. Beaton now has to explain the variations in the texts by postulating that in the vernacular tradition the function of a copyist overlaps with that of the author. There is not a shred of evidence for this in the Greek world, and Beaton has to go to 13th century France to find a lonely parallel to the copyist/author (179).

The language, on Beaton's theory, is a literary *Kunstsprache*, not an oral one. The mixture of forms, on his view, is the result of a conscious effort by the scribe-poets. We would object that we know too little about what actually is in the manuscripts to be able to say much about the actual linguistic *Variationsbreite*; moreover, this lack of linguistic conformity should be explained with reference to the living language, in which simultaneous existence of different forms would not be remarkable. We are at present not able to say what is 'art' and what is linguistic 'reality' in the vernacular texts. Much more work needs to be done on the manuscripts and the texts, before we will be able to formulate on a secure basis the broad generalizations of which there are too many in Beaton's book.

Recently, also the Jeffreys have raised the problem of lack of adequate modern editions.[250] Their ideas, however, of what a modern critical edition should be, are based on conceptions derived from their work on the *War of Troy*, which we would not find applicable in neither the *Livistros* nor the *Achilleid.* In fact, the manuscripts containing vernacular texts have so far received very little attention. For a number of these manuscripts we do have modern and reliable descriptions, but they are clearly in a minority. Very little work has been done on the identification of the scribes, and published information about the manuscripts can be found to be misleading and imprecise. Since so much depends on incontrovertible evidence from the manuscripts, one might have expected that scholars had addressed themselves more vigorously to this important field. Chatzigiakoumis, for example, who has made available a lot of information about the manuscripts, raises the question whether almost all of the manuscripts containing the

---

[250] Cf. their article in *Okeanos* 342.

romances were written in the West. From our experience we would say that he is probably right in thinking that most of them (but not all) were. If so, the further question must be raised for whom were they written? For manuscript collectors? For the Greek public in Italy? It should be stressed, however, that Chatzigiakoumis did not pretend to have dealt with these problems at all. There is a danger that his off-hand judgments are accepted as proved without further research.[251]

At the beginning of the present chapter Beaton correctly states that the problem of the manuscript transmission is crucial to the whole subject of the chapter, but he never, as far as we can see, comes to the heart of the matter: that there is no manuscript transmission as we know it for the classical and learned Byzantine texts. For the translated texts, the Jeffreys may be right that something like a textual history of the *War of Troy* can be constructed (we have to judge this point when the edition appears) so that we can justifiably argue that all surviving manuscripts go back to a common source, the original translation of Benoît's poem. But in the case of the *Imberios* we cannot be so certain, at least not to judge from the MSS.[252] The same applies to the text of *Florios*, known from two widely divergent MSS. Also in the *Theseid* we seem to have two witnesses that are not so easy to handle, unless it turns out to be correct that the Paris MS was the source of the Vatican which ended up as the printers' copy for the φυλλάδιο. For the other vernacular texts we have different versions which cannot be put into the strait-jacket of a traditional Lachmannian stemma. For example, it makes no sense to attempt to establish a stemma for the three MSS of the *Achilleid*; we would not be able to reach a common source in that way, an original *Achilleid*, so that we could use the stemma to decide the text of the original. And perhaps it is the point here to stress a truth forgotten all too often: a stemma in the Maasian sense (the sense in which most, if not all historians of medieval texts use the concept) is not just a symbol of how things might have happened, but a never failing method (except where contamination comes in) to decide

---

[251] Cf. the Jeffreys' unqualified statements *Okeanos* 341.

[252] Perhaps we should mention here that H. Schreiner's attempt to establish a stemma for the *Imberios* (*Akten des XI. Byzantinistenkongresses München 1958* [München 1960] 556-562) does not convince in the least; nor does his quaint idea that **N** contains traces of the Catalan text (**N** 483, f. 88r). M. Pichard, REB 10 (1952) 91f rejects the evidence for a Catalan origin without mentioning explicitly this particular passage from **N**.

what was in the archetype that we are reconstructing.[253]

---

[253] By pointing out this basic principle we have not committed ourselves to a belief in Maasian stemmatics; we would rather subscribe to Pasquali's views (set forth with great learning in *Storia della tradizione e critica del testo* [2. ed. Firenze 1962] following his review of Maas in Gnomon 5 [1929] 417-435 and 498-521), especially in view of what has happened in the transmission of most classical authors, namely that the MSS have been infested by the very infection against which Maas (*Textkritik* [3. Auflage Leipzig 1957] 31) warned that 'kein Kraut gewachsen ist': contamination. But we should like to see a Maasian stemma used the way it was meant to be used, not just as an illustration paying lip-service to a little understood strict and logical construct.

Chapter 12

Reception

In this last chapter of his book Beaton first discusses the contemporary public, and secondly, the way in which the romances were read and received in later literature.[254]

The discussion of the intended public is very confused, to put it mildly, because Beaton does not distinguish very clearly between fictional-rhetorical *topoi* and the social reality. Further, he attempts to look for evidence about the public in the texts which makes him reconstruct the real world on the basis of fictional conventions.

In discussing the evidence in the texts themselves for the presupposed readers/listeners, Beaton says (184) that the picture is very confused, that it seems difficult to be certain whether hearers or readers are assumed, or whether a single person or a plurality is addressed.

In the Naples *Achilleid* Beaton claims (185) that whereas the prologue implies a plurality of listeners, the narrative elsewhere addresses a single person. The evidence for a single person turns out to be authorial asides of the type νὰ εἶδες / νὰ εἶπες. But these formal phrases cannot be taken to imply what Beaton assumes. They do not suggest a single listener or reader, they just imply that the message of the text is directed at somebody.[255] And of course they cannot tell us anything about the intended public, whether they are listeners or readers. The prologue, however, is obviously addressing a plurality of listeners:

        Ἀλλ' ὅσοι καὶ ἂν αἰστάνεσθε τὸν πόθον τῶν Ἐρώτων,
10   ὅσοι ἂν οὐκ ἐδέξασθε τρῶσιν ποσῶς ἀγάπης,
        ἅπαντες νῦν ἀκούσατε τὴν ἀφήγησιν τὴν ταύτην,
        τὴν ὑπερποθουερωτικὴν καὶ ποθουπονεμένη,
        νὰ μάθετε δὲ ἅπαντες, νὰ πληροφορηθῆτε,
        τὸ πῶς ὁ πόθος δύναται καὶ πόσα καταφλέγει,

---

[254] We omit from our discussion Beaton's recent article 'Orality and the reception of late Byzantine vernacular literature', BMGS 14 (1990) 174-184, since it repeats in even more condensed and therefore distorted form what he says in this chapter.

[255] Like the type of abstract singular in the case of German 'man'.

15   νὰ μάθετε τὴν δύναμιν καὶ τὴν ἰσχὺν τὴν ἔχει,
        νὰ μάθετε τὰ τόξα τους καὶ νὰ τοὺς προσκυνῆτε,
        καὶ νὰ μὴ ἀλαζονεύεσθε πρὸς τὴν φρικτὴν τὴν τόλμην,
        αὐθέντας νὰ τοὺς ἔχετε καὶ νὰ τοὺς προσκυνῆτε,
        ὅτι φρικτὸς καὶ θαυμαστὸς καὶ μέγας ρήγας ἔναι.[256]

For the *Belthandros* the evidence points the same way. There are the usual formal asides (e.g. νὰ εἶπες 453) which do not prove anything, and a prologue

        Δεῦτε, προσκαρτερήσατε μικρόν, ὦ νέοι πάντες·
        θέλω σᾶς ἀφηγήσασθαι λόγους ὡραιωτάτους
3   ὑπόθεσιν παράξενην, πολλὰ παρηλλαγμένην

addressed to a plurality of listeners. In the *Byzantine Iliad*, Beaton (185) finds a single listener addressed in lines 1110-1111, against the plurality of young people referred to elsewhere (887). In fact the picture is somewhat different. The single listener here can be regarded as of the same type as the single listener in the formalised asides, whereas the young people who are referred to not only once, are the prospective audience for which the author is writing his didactic poem. As far as we can see there is a fairly stable picture. The Oxford version of the *Achilleid* which otherwise fits into this general frame, referring to a single listener in the formal asides (νὰ εἶδες 184, 268, 422: ἄκου 661), contains a solitary exception in that we there find a plural in an authorial aside line 566 (λέγω σας). The translations seem to conform to the above; in the *Florios* the singular is kept throughout in the authorial asides (cf. lines 111, 276, 646, 1391 and 1591), but in this text there is no address to a plurality of listeners.

In order to understand the rhetoric in the references we have to distinguish between the formalised asides, which as a rule are in the second person singular denoting a generalizing indefinite personal subject, and the addresses or references to the plurality of listeners for whom the text is intended. There is no need to see a discrepancy here between a single person and a plurality; the two categories are on different levels. One might also doubt *a priori* whether it would be sociologically meaningful to imagine these texts addressed to single listeners or hearers. The confusion Beaton finds here derives from his own wrong approach to the formalities of the genre. He attempts to explain the differences between the texts by assuming a distinction between older and later texts. Thus he finds a similar relation between author and audience in the

---

[256] The text is taken from Ole L. Smith's forthcoming edition of the Naples version of the *Achilleid*. The reader using Hesseling's edition will see that Smith's text differs from Hesseling's by going back to the MS.

interpolated end of the *Achilleid*, in the prologue to the *Belthandros* (which he regards as a later interpolation) and in the *Byzantine Iliad*. The futility of this distinction between older and supposedly later texts is obvious from the prologue to the Naples *Achilleid* (by Beaton's own admission probably the oldest of the surviving romances), where we find the same situation: a young audience addressed with more or less explicit didactic intentions, as in the *Belthandros*.

However, there is a dangerous point here which should be emphasized. Beaton endeavours to support his theory by referring to Chatzigiakoumis' somewhat apodictic claim[257] that most of our manuscripts were copied during the century after the fall of Byzantium, and that the motive behind this copying was the preservation and dissemination of a dying heritage. The more didactic the fictional situation, Beaton argues, the later the text. The last point we may not take seriously. But there has been a tendency after the publication of Chatzigiakoumis' book to regard his final summarizing remarks as far more authoritative than the evidence adduced allows.[258] We need, as we have stressed, much more work on the manuscripts, including of course the problem of their date, before we can venture to say anything definite about the majority having been written in the West or about their intended public and purpose.

Apart from the *Kallimachos*, then, Beaton (186) finds that the texts are unable to decide what public they are addressing. He therefore proposes to look for narrating situations in the texts themselves, although one would think that this was a wholly different and not at all comparable matter. He finds the 'ideal' audience described in *Kallimachos* 852-859, and then claims (187) that this audience, a single king, is a far cry from the indiscriminate young audiences assumed by the *Belthandros* proem and the *Byzantine Iliad* (we have seen above that references to a young public in the *Byzantine Iliad* are references to an intended fictional audience). We would protest against this lack of method that will draw conclusions from the fictional to the real situation. In this development from a very small public of high social standing to a larger and less educated one, Beaton recognizes the actual development of the audience of the romance, and by a misinterpretation of the end of the *Livistros* (on which see above p. 67) he finds proof in the texts for his view (188).

A final remark on the intended audience in the *Byzantine Iliad*. The author

---

[257] *Op. cit.* 247.

[258] See our comments above p. 100. We should add here that the readiness with which some of Chatzigiakoumis' less compelling ideas have been accepted, contrasts sharply with the fact that his basic messages, the unreliability of our editions and the need for going back to the MSS, have been less acclaimed. Lynda Garland in her recent paper on sexuality in the romances (see above n. 148) completely ignores Chatzigiakoumis' work.

emphasizes his inadequacy to deal with this vast subject in competition with Homer, and excuses himself on the grounds that he has a young audience in mind who needs to be told about the world and the instability of human existence. We should be aware that this is a rhetorical device. This argument is adduced three times: lines 493-496

ἀλλ' ὅμως ἀπὸ τὰ πολλὰ τὰ ἀρίθμητα ἐκεῖνα
τίποτ' ἐλέξομαι μικρὸν τινὰς εἰς νεωτέρους,
495 καὶ νὰ ἐγνωρίζουν ἅπαντες τὸν πλανωμένον κόσμον
τὸν ἄστατον, ἀκέρδητον, τοὺς ἅπαντας κομπώνει.

lines 886-888

ἡμεῖς δὲ βίβλους ἔχομεν σοφῶν τε καὶ ῥητόρων
ἀλλ' ὅμως γράφω παιδινὰ τινὰς τῶν νεωτέρων,
τάχα μικρὸν νὰ ἐγροικοῦ τὴν ἱστορίαν τῆς Τροίας.

and lines 1060-1071

1060 ἡμεῖς γάρ τι παραμικρὸν τὸ κατὰ τῆς δυνάμης
εἰς ἰδιώτας παιδινὰ γράφω τὰ τῆς Τρωάδος,
ὅπως γνωρίζουν ἅπαντες τὰ πράγματα τοῦ κόσμου,
οὔτε τὰ κάλλη ὀφελοῦν οὔτε ὁ πλοῦτος μένει
1065 οὔτε ἀνδρεία δύναται θάνατον πολεμῆσαι,
τὰ πάντα μάταια κενά, τὰ πάντα ζοφωμένα,
πλάνη μεγάλη θαυμαστὴ στὴν ἀνθρωπείαν φύσιν,
καὶ τὸ μυστήριον τὸ φρικτὸν κανεὶς οὐκ ἐνθυμᾶται,
1070 ἀλλὰ τὰ μάταια καὶ κενὰ σπουδάζουν καὶ μοχθοῦσιν,
πλεονεξίαν καὶ ἁρπαγήν, φθόνον, ἀλαζονίαν.

He introduces, moreover, the subject of Achilles with whom he will deal though the subject has been covered by Homer (795-799):

795 θέλω μικρὸν ν' ἀφηγηθῶ μεγάλου Ἀχιλλέως,
ὥσπερ ἄγαν φιλόσοφος Ὅμηρος διδασκάλων
ὁ ποιητὴς ὁ θαυμαστὸς τὰ τῶν Ἑλλήνων πάθη,
αὐτὸς βιβλίον ἱστόρησε μεγάλου Ἀχιλλέως
τὰς πράξεις καὶ τὰς ἀρετὰς καὶ τὰ χαρίσματά του.

Beaton (185) takes the similarity with the *Imberios* [259] and the interpolated end of the Naples *Achilleid* [260] to be significant for the dating: they are all late, he argues, from about

---

[259] He does not refer to any particular passage, but says that the relation to the hearers is repeated in almost identical terms.
[260] Nor is there any precise reference to this text, but he is presumably thinking of lines 1798ff which we quote below.

the mid-fifteenth century, and thus strengthen his case for the didactic tendency he tries to establish. Perhaps they are late and perhaps they have a didactic scope, but we should be aware that the passage in the *Achilleid* **N** is both equally rhetorical and also somewhat different from the *Byz. II.* passages with which it has no more than a superficial similarity:

    Ἡμεῖς δὲ βίβλοις ποιητῶν, σοφῶν τε καὶ ῥητόρων
    καὶ φιλοσόφων παλαιῶν, μεγάλων διδασκάλων,
1800 Ὁμήρου πρώτου τῶν σοφῶν καὶ ποιητοῦ μεγάλου
    Ἀριστοτέλου, Πλάτωνος ἢ λέγω Παλαμήδη,
    ἀναγινώσκοντες ἀεὶ λόγου παιδείας χάριν,
    παρεξεβάλομεν αὐτὴν διήγησιν τοῦ Ἀχιλλέως
    καὶ μετεβάλομεν αὐτὴν εἰς σαφεστέραν ῥῆσιν,
1805 ὅπως γνωρίζουν οἱ πολλοί, οἱ μὴ μαθόντες λόγους,
    τὴν γέννησιν, ἀνατροφήν, ἀνδρεία τοῦ Ἀχιλλέως
    καὶ πῶς ἐπῆρεν τὴν ὡραιὰν ἐκείνην τὴν κουρτέσαν,
    εἶτα τὸν ταύτης θάνατον, τὴν συμφορὰν ἐκείνην
    καὶ τελευταῖον τὸν ἄδικον θάνατον τοῦ Ἀχιλλέως.
1810 Καὶ οἱ ἀναγινώσκοντες τὴν ἱστορίαν ταύτην
    μάθετε πῶς παρέρχουνται τὰ πράγματα τοῦ κόσμου.

The author of the **N** *Achilleid* is here very explicit about what he has done: he has made classical literature accessible to a broader audience (not specifically young people) through a change of linguistic register (**N** 1804). Far from suggesting dependence, the rhetoric in the two texts is thus wholly different.

Beaton then goes on to deal with what he calls 'literary reception' (189). From his discussion it appears that the 'reception' he is considering is neither 19th century *Rezeptionsgeschichte* nor *Rezeptionsästhetik* in the Jaussian sense. More truthfully it could probably be called parallelhunting in later narrative texts, or investigation of certified cases of impact. He laments the fact that not much work has been done in this field (190), and unfortunately his own treatment of it shows why: there is almost no material of a sort that scholars of sober disposition and respect for the difference between the provable and unprovable would like to handle.

The first section deals with Byzantine court poetry and starts with a discussion of the celebrated case of Manuel Philes' poem, assumed to be an allegorical interpretation of the *Kallimachos*. According to Beaton (191) there can be no doubt at all that the book of love Philes is interpreting is the *Kallimachos*. Not very plausibly Beaton suggests that the 'small discrepancies between Filís' résumé and the romance as we know it might possibly be due to the transmission of the text of the latter' (191), as if we had any reason to suspect that something was missing in the *Kallimachos* text as transmitted, and he continues with an even more unsound argument 'but Filís is selective in choosing those elements of the plot that will sustain his allegorical reading' (*ibid.*). With some reason one might ask how we can know anything about Philes' selection, unless we have already decided that we are dealing with the *Kallimachos*? The fair summary of Philes' poem shows to our mind that the reader, provided that one is determined to look upon the problem with an open mind, is here given the evidence in hand why Philes cannot be writing about the *Kallimachos*. What Philes' poem may be taken as indicating, is the social accept of the genre at the imperial court at the time.

Philes' imaginative allegorical interpretation cannot, of course, be accepted today, and there is no use discussing it at length, within the framework of a modern approach to Byzantine literature. But the importance of his reading is, as Beaton correctly points out, that this is one of the very few texts that gives evidence about how the educated Byzantines at the time were prepared to read the romances. Nor is there any reason to wonder why Philes was able to misinterpret the romance in the way he probably did, for allegorical interpretation is one of the standard Byzantine (and medieval in general) reactions to pagan literature, witness the allegorical interpretation of Homer, of the pagan myths and of the ancient novel.

Now there is more to the allegorical interpretation than that, for when one further attempts to find in the last lines of the romance a sort of pointer towards an interpretation on the spiritual level with the mention of God's graces, we are almost certainly on slippery ground. There is no indication in the text - apart from this one line - that we are allowed to read this as a specifically Christian 'redemption'. Nor is Beaton prepared to take the pious sentiments with which the romance ends in lines 2606-2607 as anything more than conventional piety (234 n. 10), which he moreover tries to put at the copyist's door. Though mistaken, we think that this attempt raises much more fundamental problems about the 'reception' of the romances. Beaton (192) touches upon the matter in his final remarks about Philes being nearer to the expectations of the fourteenth century reader, than is immediately apparent today. This point is not taken up elsewhere, as far as we can see. It raises, however, the problem of the relation between author and public in a way that Beaton does not seem to make explicit. If it is possible to say anything about the expectations of the audience, in what way do they affect the author and his work? And should we distinguish between the expectations of different social classes among the public? Are we trying to reconstruct the 'historical' meaning(s) of the romances, or are we intent upon making them into literary texts in no specific time and space, accessible to the modern reader without thought for how they were read or interpreted by the public for whom they were written, and whose expectations they should be thought of as reacting to? These vital questions have not been dealt with by Beaton in a methodical way.

The great difficulty in dealing with the literary reception - in Beaton's terms - of the romance appears clearly in connection with Meliteniotes' *To Chastity*. There are practically no certain allusions to specific romances; the quality of the proofs adduced for Meliteniotes' use of the romances may be exemplified by the reference to the use of first-person narrative (195) which is said to be an allusion to the *Livistros*. This should deceive no one, nor should one accept the *non sequitur* that since Meliteniotes seems to be referring to, among other texts, also Western literature, this strengthens the argument that the Constantinopolitan writers of romance, whose works he parodies, were more steeped in the comparable literature of the West than they overtly confess (*ibid.*).[261]

Similarly inconclusive is the appearance of romance *topoi* in the Περὶ Δυστυχίας καὶ Εὐτυχίας. Neither the folkloric material, the castles and the μύθος ἔρωτος in the interpolated Leipzig version can be seen as anything else but vague references to the romances.[262]

The same can be said for the *Belisarios*, irrespective of whether one accepts the case argued by Bakker and van Gemert of this text's having been heavily interpolated at several stages from the *Achilleid* and the *Imberios*, which if true happened not on the authorial level but in the manuscript(s) from which the extant Naples manuscript is descended.

At first sight the 15th century Z version of the *Digenis* looks more promising (198f). Here we find a considerable amount of motifs well known from existing romances, and if Michael Jeffreys is right in concluding that the author of this compilation worked from *Digenis* MSS extant today, there is a presumption that his sources for the first book of the Z version may be found among our extant romance MSS. Now, there are many similarities, but nothing really compelling. The compiler may have derived words and phrases from the extant romances (some of this material can be found in Trapp's apparatus of parallels); in no case can we establish the exact source.

---

[261] See our objections above p. 81.

[262] On this text see Beck, *Geschichte* 147-148. A new edition is being prepared by Maria Politi-Sakellariadi, cf. her paper in H. Eideneier (ed.), *Neograeca medii aevi* 285-293.

This state of affairs would suggest that the author of the compilation was a bit more independent than Jeffreys implies. To speak of an original composition would perhaps be to overstate the case, though on Beaton's view there is no difference between the **Z** compiler Eustathios and the anonymous author of the *Byzantine Iliad*: their works are both of them collages of incoherent material.

However, there is one point in Beaton's analysis of this text that merits a fuller discussion. In the prologue to the first book of **Z** Beaton finds part of the explanation for so many of our manuscripts' dating from after the fall of Constantinople: there was a demand, 'the compiler tells us, among a public not especially educated, to preserve these stories' (200). We submit that this does not follow from the prologue:

> Τέκνον μου ποθεινότατον καὶ προσφιλέστατόν μου,
> πολλάκις με ἠξίωσας πάσας τὰς κατορθώσεις
> διὰ γραφῆς δηλῶσαι σοι τοῦ Διγενοῦς Ἀκρίτου,
> καὶ σοῦ τὸν λόγον ἤκουσα ἐκδυσωπήσαντός με
> 5 καὶ παρευθὺς ἐκίνησα καὶ ἄρχισα νὰ γράφω
> ἅπαντα τὰ τοῦ Διγενοῦς καὶ τῶν αὐτοῦ γονέων
> κατορθώματα θαυμαστὰ πραχθέντα ἐξ ἐκείνων.

There is not a word to support the far-reaching inferences that Beaton pulls out of this prologue, and it may even be held that he misinterprets the first three lines whose topicality is rather obvious. There is more to come, for Beaton then goes on to find proof of his would-be author/scribe in the author of this compilation (200):

> 'the activity in which this 'forger' has been detected gives the strongest proof yet of the overlap in function between authors and copyists: a copyist finding a lacuna in the text before him apparently sees nothing unusual, still less reprehensible, in filling it with a composition of his own.

Now, Eustathios was not a 'scribe'. And what he did cannot be compared to what Beaton, among others, thinks that scribes have been doing in the manuscripts of the *Achilleid* and the *Belisarios*, namely to change words in their sources for no obvious reasons, to add lines they knew from elsewhere to the text they were copying - again for no reason, and to throw out lines and passages as they happened to please. And for Beaton's third point in relation to the **Z** version that it shows to what extent the genre 'had become standard fare for copyists and presumably also for readers and audiences' is not evident to us, since other texts have also been dated to the fifteenth century without being regarded as especially indicative for the menu of copyists, standard or not. And there is still no evidence that Eustathios was a copyist, no more than the author of the *Byzantine Iliad*.

Finally, we come down to Cretan literature which not surprisingly has even less to offer. The lengths of special pleading to which Beaton is prepared to go here in order to find and highlight the most inconclusive shred of evidence can be gathered from his mention of one of the manuscripts containing Falieros' poems (203) 'the notorious Naples manuscript that also includes the *Tale of Achilles*, *Belisarios* and *Imberios*'; but he adds self-defeatingly, 'although Falieros' poems were bound into it some decades after the copying of these texts.' He might have added that the Falieros part in the Naples manuscript is written by another hand and has separate counting of gatherings. So why use this as evidence for early sixteenth century scribes' recognition of Falieros' dependence on the romance? And, we might ask, what is the significance or importance of views of sixteenth century scribes who were working for Western MSS collectors? It is also interesting to notice that the Naples manuscript which elsewhere in Beaton's book belonged to the last quarter of the fifteenth century, here seems to get assigned to the sixteenth century. Or is the reader presumed to be aware that the part containing Falieros can be dated from watermarks to the first decades of the sixteenth century?[263] The manuscript containing Falieros together with Makrembolites, a coupling which Beaton finds particularly significant, was written by Andronikos Noukios around 1541-1544,[264] and thus rather by a scholar who was also a professional copyist. And by all means, Noukios as everyone else copying these romance texts copied them together with similar texts, which does not imply any specific idea of literary dependence; this had something to with the way in which these texts were regarded, as a category to themselves. There is, moreover, nothing unusual in this, and the student of textual history will remember several examples of texts following each other in the MSS.[265]

All this is not to deny the relations between Falieros and older literature. We certainly think that there is good sense in reading Falieros on a background of 12th century and vernacular romance, just as there is good sense in seeing an Italian Renaissance lyric poetry background. But to try to pin down the single elements in Falieros and find their origin in specific texts in the way Beaton has done it is not contributing to a methodologically sound theory of literary reception.

---

[263] See A. van Gemert's edition of Falieros 50 (cf. above n. 123).

[264] Probably; van Gemert thinks this was copied while Noukios was still living in Korfu, that is before 1537. For this scribe see now the material collected in Ernst Gamillscheg & Dieter Harlfinger, *Repertorium der griechischen Kopisten 800-1600. 1.Teil. Grossbritannien.* (Wien 1981) A. Nr. 20 , supplemented in *2.Teil. Frankreich.* (Wien 1989) A. Nr. 27 .

[265] We may refer to the way in which classical texts commented upon by Manuel Moschopoulos tend to be transmitted together. Alexander Turyn's series of studies on the transmission of the tragedians have shown that texts like Hesiod or Pindar with Moschopulean scholia are often transmitted together with one or more of the dramatists.

At the end of this most inconclusive chapter we are treated to some airy speculations about Kornaros and the *Erotokritos* which we find one should better leave alone. The interested reader will find a particularly unconvincing piece of reasoning (206-207) where Beaton manages to contradict himself by admitting that Holton has shown that all that Kornaros could have known of Greek vernacular literature on first hand were the printed texts of the *Theseid* and of the rhymed version of the *Imberios*.[266]

---

[266] On Kornaros' probable knowledge of Greek vernacular texts see David Holton's analysis in R. Beaton (ed.), *The Greek Novel AD 1-1985* (London 1988) 144-153. There is not much to go upon, and Holton is even sceptical about Kornaros' presumed (by Gareth Morgan) use of the *Theseid*.

Epilogue

At the beginning of the present study we promised to return to the question whether Beaton had succeeded in his attempt or not. It will not come as a surprise to the reader who has had the patience of going through the preceding pages that we do not think that he has accomplished his goal of writing a book of the kind he had envisaged.

In this sense we cannot possibly agree with G. Kehagioglou's opinion that Beaton's monograph is 'ένα από τα πιο αξιόλογα βιβλία των τριάντα τελευταίων χρόνων'.[267]

It will not come as a surprise that in our opinion the time has not yet come to write a broad study for the general reader and specialist alike, on the Byzantine romance. Too many of the basic problems need further discussion and clarification; we have tried to point to and discuss some of the most important, but we would be the first to admit that our covering of the ground has left other critical issues almost untouched.

What we have tried to do here, is partly to issue a warning against an approach to a central part of Byzantine studies that we find too facile, partly to reemphasize where in our opinion the most fruitful and rewarding fields for research are to be found:

1) The careful and detailed study of the manuscripts transmitting learned and vernacular romances, a study which would have to include full palaeographical and codicological investigations, as well as a comparison with the rest of Byzantine and post-byzantine bookproduction; 2) linguistic and stylistic analysis of the texts involved; 3) critical editions according to the latest standards of textual criticism, with the peculiarity and complexity of vernacular texts in mind; 4) comparative studies with the available oral material and Arabic/Persian romance writing; 5) clarification of a sound methodology of literary analysis based on a better understanding of both Byzantine poetics and modern literary theory. These directions of research are more needed in our field than attempts at summarizing in a fashion that leads the reader to believe that there are no dangers around for the unwary, that our studies have progressed so far that books like

---

[267] See his review in Ελληνικά 41 (1990) 158-171, the quotation from p. 171. It is unfortunate that Kehagioglou, beyond his justified criticism of Beaton's omission of non-erotic texts and Oriental comparative material, praises the author's αναμφισβήτητη φιλολογική οξύνοια (p.165) and considers chapters 10-12 as the most original contributions in the book (p.167). For example, his exposition of ch. 10 (pp.167-168), which we consider one of Beaton's worst, lacks any argumentative foundation for his agreements and/or objections. One correction: the first motto in Beaton's book is referred to as 'της κριτικού E. Waugh' (p.159). It is, of course, a passage from a work by the male(!) English author Evelyn Waugh (1903-1966), famous for such novels as *Scoop* (1938), *Brideshead Revisited* (1945) and *The Loved One* (1948).

Beaton's can be written without conveying false impressions.

Even in an area as limited as ours the days are long past when masters like Krumbacher and Beck could overlook it in its entirety. Today things have become too complex - which of course is a good sign that we have progressed - and no single Byzantinist or Neohellenist can dream of writing the synthesis that will give an adequate presentation of every corner of the whole area from codicology to literary criticism, from the 10th to the 17th century, from the *Digenis* to the *Erotokritos*.

BIBLIOGRAPHY

Panagiotis A. Agapitos, 'Michael Italikos, Klage auf den Tod seines Rebhuhns', BZ 82 (1989) 59-68.

- , ' Ἡ εἰκόνα τοῦ αὐτοκράτορα Βασιλείου Α΄ στὴν φιλομακεδονικὴ γραμματεία 867-959'. Ἑλληνικά 40 (1989) 285-322.

- , 'The Erotic Bath in the Byzantine Vernacular Romance *Kallimachos and Chrysorrhoe*, ClMed 41 (1990) 257-273.

- , 'Textkritisches zu *Kallimachos und Chrysorrhoe*', Ἑλληνικά 41 (1990) 33-41.

- , *Narrative Structure in the Byzantine Vernacular Romances. A Textual and Literary Study of Kallimachos, Belthandros and Libistros* [Miscellanea Byzantina Monacensia 33] (München 1991).

- , 'Byzantine Literature and Greek Philologists in the Nineteenth Century', ClMed 43 (1992) [forthcoming].

- , '*Libistros und Rhodamne*: Vorläufiges zu einer kritischen Ausgabe der Version A', JÖB 42 (1992) [forthcoming].

A. D. Aleksidze, *Mir grečeskogo rycarskogo romana (XIII-XIV vv.)* (Tbilisi 1979).

Margaret Alexiou, 'Modern Greek Folklore and its Relation to the Past: the Evolution of Charos in Greek Tradition', in: S.Vryonis (ed.): *Βυζαντινά καὶ Μεταβυζαντινά 1* (Malibu 1978) 221-236.

- , 'The Poverty of Écriture and the Craft of Writing: Towards a Reappraisal of the Prodromic Poems', BMGS 10 (1986) 1-40.

Margaret Alexiou - David Holton, 'The origins and development of "politikos stichos"', Μαντατοφόρος 9 (1976) 22-34.

St. Alexiou, '*Ἀπόκοπος*', Κρητικὰ Χρονικά 17 (1963) 183-251.

- , review of **Promponas**, Ἀκριτικά, Ἑλληνικά 39 (1988) 189-195.

- , *Βασίλειος Διγενὴς Ἀκρίτης καὶ Τὸ ᾆσμα τοῦ Ἀρμούρη. Κριτικὴ ἔκδοση* [Φιλολογικὴ βιβλιοθήκη 5] (Athens 1985).

G. De Andrés, *Catálogo de los códices griegos de la Real Biblioteca de El Escorial* III (Madrid 1967).

Ph. Apostolopoulos, *La langue du roman byzantin 'Callimaque et Chrysorrhoé'* [Diss. Paris IV-Sorbonne 1972] (Athens 1984).

Wim F. Bakker - Arnold van Gemert. Ἱστορία τοῦ Βελισαρίου. Κριτικὴ ἔκδοση τῶν τεσσάρων διασκευῶν μὲ εἰσαγωγή, σχόλια καὶ γλωσσάριο [Βυζαντινὴ καὶ νεοελληνικὴ βιβλιοθήκη 6] (Athens 1988).

Shadi Bartsch, *Decoding the Ancient Novel. The Reader and the Role of Description in Heliodorus and Achilles Tatius* (Princeton, N. J. 1989).

R. Beaton, 'Orality and the Reception of Late Byzantine Vernacular Literature', BMGS 14 (1990) 174-184.

H.-G. Beck, *Theodoros Metochites. Die Krise des byzantinischen Weltbildes im 14. Jahrhundert* (München 1952).

- , 'Byzantinische Literatur. 3. Die Volksliteratur', in: *Geschichte der Textüberlieferung der antiken und mittelalterlichen Literatur.* Band I (Zürich 1961) 470-493.

- , *Geschichte der byzantinischen Volksliteratur* [Handbuch der Altertumswissenschaft xii, 2.3] (München 1971).

- , *Das literarische Schaffen der Byzantiner. Wege zu seinem Verständnis* [Sitzungsberichte der Österreichischen Akademie der Wissenschaften, philol.-hist. Klasse, 229. 4] (Wien 1974).

_ , 'Die griechische volkstümliche Literatur des 14. Jahrhunderts. Eine Standortsbestimmung', *Actes du XIVe Congrès International des Études Byzantines (Bucarest, 6-12 Septembre 1971)*, publiés par les soins de M. Berza et E. Stanescu, Vol. I (Bucarest 1974) 125-138.

- ,'Der Leserkreis der byzantinischen 'Volksliteratur' im Licht der handschriftlichen Überlieferung', *Byzantine Books and Bookmen* [Dumbarton Oaks Colloquium 1971] (Dumbarton Oaks 1975) 47-67.

- , *Das byzantinische Jahrtausend* (München 1978).

- , *Byzantinisches Erotikon* (München 1986).

- , 'Ortodossia ed erotismo. Marginalia alla letteratura erotica bizantina', in: H.-G. Beck - F. Conca - Carolina Cupane, *Il romanzo tra cultura latina e cultura bizantina.* Testi della III settimana residenziale di studi medievali (Carini, Villa Belvedere, 17-21 Ottobre 1983), a cura di C. Roccaro [Biblioteca del' Enchiridion 5] (Palermo 1986) 13-32.

P. Hildebrand Beck O.S.B. (= H.-G. Beck), *Vorsehung und Vorherbestimmung in der theologischen Literatur der Byzantiner* [Orientalia Christiana Analecta 114] (Roma 1937).

A. Zimbone di Benedetto, 'Il *Roman de Troie* di Benoit de Saint-Maure e la ricostituzione del testo del Πόλεμος τῆς Τρωάδος', Siculorum Gymnasium 30 (1977) 225-244.

F. Boulenger (ed.), St. Basile, Πρὸς τοὺς νέους ὅπως ἂν ἐξ ἑλληνικῶν ὠφέλοιντο λόγων (Paris 1935).

E. L. Bowie, 'The Greek Novel', in: P. E. Easterling - B. M. W. Knox, *The Cambridge History of Classical Literature vol. I. Greek Literature* (Cambridge 1985) 683-699.

Robert Browning, *Studies on Byzantine History, Literature and Education* (Variorum

Reprints, London 1977).

- , *Medieval and Modern Greek* (2. ed., Cambridge 1983).

A. Bryer, 'The first encounter with the West, A.D.1050-1204', in: P. Whitting (ed.), *Byzantium: an Introduction* (Oxford 1981) 83-110.

Eva Cantarella, 'Dangling virgins: Myth, Ritual and the Place of Women in Ancient Greece' in: Susan Rubin Suleiman (ed.),: *The Female Body in Western Culture. Contemporary Perspectives* (Cambridge, Mass.- London 1987) 57-67.

B. Cerquiglini, *Éloge de la variante. Histoire critique de la philologie* (Paris 1989).

- , 'Variantes d'auteur et variance de copiste', in: L. Hay (ed.),: *La naissance du texte* (Paris 1989) 105-119.

M. K. Chatzigiakoumis. Τὰ μεσαιωνικὰ δημώδη κείμενα. Συμβολή στὴ μελέτη καὶ τὴν ἔκδοσή τους. Αʹ : Λίβιστρος, Καλλίμαχος, Βέλθανδρος (Athens 1977).

J. C. Cheynet, 'Mantzikert: un désastre militaire?', Byzantion 50 (1980) 410-438.

D. Claude, *Die byzantinische Stadt im 6.Jahrhundert* [Byzantinisches Archiv 13] (München 1969).

Vincenzo Crescini (ed.), *Il Cantare di Fiorio e Biancifiore* edito ed illustrato da Vincenzo Crescini vol.ii [Scelta di curiosità letterarie inedite o rare dal secolo xiii al xvii in appendice alla Collezione di opere inedite o rare. Dispensa ccii] (Bologna 1899).

Carolina Cupane, ' "Ἔρως βασιλεύς. La figura di Eros nel romanzo d'amore', Atti dell' Academia di scienze, lettere e arti di Palermo, Ser. iv 33.2.2 (1974) 243-297.

- , 'Il motivo del castello nella narrativa tardobizantina. Evoluzione di un' allegoria' , JÖB 27 (1978) 229-267.

- , 'Topica romanzesca in oriente e in occidente: 'avanture' e 'amour'', in: H. G. Beck - F. Conca - Carolina Cupane, *Il romanzo tra cultura latina e bizantina*. Testi della III settimana residenziale di studi medievali (Carini, Villa Belvedere, 17-21 Ottobre 1983), a cura di C. Roccaro [Biblioteca dell' Encheiridion 5] (Palermo 1986) 47-72.

- , 'Byzantinisches Erotikon: Ansichten und Einsichten', JÖB 37 (1987) 213-233.

Alphonse Dain, *Les Manuscrits* (3e ed. Paris 1975).

Georg Danezis, *Spaneas: Vorlage, Quellen, Versionen* [Miscellanea Byzantina Monacensia 31] (München 1987).

Judy K. Deuling - John Cirignano, 'The Later ABS Family Manuscripts of Xenophon's *Hiero* Tradition', Scriptorium 44 (1990) 54-68.

E. R. Dodds, *The Greeks and the Irrational* [Sather Classical Lectures 25] (Berkeley 1951).

- , *Pagan and Christian in an Age of Anxiety* (Cambridge 1965).

Hans Eideneier (ed.), *Neograeca Medii Aevi. Text und Ausgabe*. Akten zum Symposion Köln 1986 [Neograeca Medii Aevi 1] (Köln 1987).

- , review of **I.Tsavari**, Südostforschungen 47 (1988) 481-483.

Hans Eideneier(Hrsg.), *Ptochoprodromos. Einführung, kritische Ausgabe, deutsche Übersetzung, Glossar* [Neograeca Medii Aevi 5] (Köln 1991).

Fabliaux. Französische Schwankererzählungen des Hochmittelalters. Ausgewählt, übersetzt und kommentiert von **A. Gier** (Stuttgart 1985) 309-313.

L. Ferry - A. Renault, *La pensée 68. Essai sur l'antihumanisme contemporain* (Paris 1988).

Suzanne Fleischman, 'Philology, Linguistics and the Discourse of the Medieval Text', Speculum 65 (1990) 19-37.

John M. Foley, *The Theory of Oral Composition* (Bloomington & Indianapolis 1988).

E. Follieri, 'La versione in greco volgare del Teseida del Boccaccio', *Atti dell' VIII Congresso internazionale di studi bizantini* (Roma 1953) 67-77.

- , *Il Teseida Neogreco. Libro I. Saggio di edizione* [Testi e Studi Bizantino-Neoellenici 1. Collezione diretta da C. Gianelli e G. Zoras] (Istituto di Studi Bizantini, Università di Roma, Roma-Atene 1959).

- , 'Su alcuni libri greci stampati a Venezia nella prima metà del cinquecento', *Contributi alla Storia del libro italiano. Miscellanea in onore di Lamberto Donati* (Firenze 1969) 119-164.

- , 'Il libro greco per i Greci nelle imprese editoriali romane e veneziane della prima metà del cinquecento', *Venezia centro di mediazione tra oriente e occidente (secoli xv-xvi). Aspetti e problemi* (Firenze 1977) 483-508.

C. Foss, *Byzantine and Turkish Sardis* (Cambridge, Mass. 1976).

C. Foss - D. Winfield, *Byzantine Fortifications. An Introduction* (Pretoria 1986).

M. Foucault, *Archéologie du savoir* (Paris 1969).

- , 'Nietzsche, genéalogie, histoire', in: *Hommage à Jean Hippolite* (Paris 1971) 145-172.

M. Fuhrmann, *Untersuchungen zur Textgeschichte der pseudo-aristotelischen Alexander-Rhetorik* [Akademie der Wissenschaften und der Literatur in Mainz, Abhandlungen der Geistes- und sozialwissenschaftlichen Klasse Jahrgang 1964, Nr. 7] (Wiesbaden 1965).

A. Fyrigos, 'Σπανίας Σπανέας. Proposta per una interpretazione del termine e ipotesi sulla datazione dell' omonimo poema', Bolletino della Badia Greca di Grottaferrata n.s. 39 (1985) 39-56.

P. Gallay, *Les manuscrits des Lettres de Saint Grégoire de Naziance* (Paris 1957).

Ernst Gamillscheg - Dieter Harlfinger, *Repertorium der griechischen Kopisten 800-1600. 1.Teil. Grossbritannien. A. Verzeichnis der Kopisten* (Wien 1981).

- , *Repertorium der griechischen Kopisten 800-1600. 2.Teil. Frankreich. A. Verzeichnis der Kopisten* (Wien 1989).

Lynda Garland, 'The "βεργὶν τρίκλωνον" of Belthandros and Chrysantza: A Note on a Popular Verse Romance and Its Sources', BZ 82 (1989) 87-95.

- , '"Be Amorous, But Be Chaste...": Sexual Morality in Byzantine Learned and Vernacular Romance', BMGS 14 (1990) 62-120.

G. Genette, 'Discours du récit. Essai de méthode', in: id., *Figures iii* (Paris 1972).

- , *Nouveau discours du récit* (Paris 1983).

- , *Mimologiques. Voyage en Cratylie* (Paris 1976).

G. Giatromanolakis (ed.), Ἀχιλλέως Ἀλεξανδρέως Τατίου Λευκίππη καὶ Κλειτοφῶν (Athens 1990).

Griechische Handschriften und Aldinen. Eine Ausstellung anlässlich der XV. Tagung der Mommsen-Gesellschaft in der Herzog August Bibliothek Wolfenbüttel (Herzog August Bibliothek Wolfenbüttel Mai 1978).

V. Grumel, *La chronologie* (Paris 1958).

G. E. von Grunebaum, *Der Islam im Mittelalter* (Zürich-Stuttgart^3 1963).

B. Haag, *Die Londoner Version der byzantinischen Achilleis* (Diss. München 1919).

Ph. Hamon, *Introduction à l'analyse du descriptif* (Paris 1981).

- , 'Rhetorical Status of the Descriptive', Yale French Studies 61 (1981) 1-26.

W. Haubrichs, 'Einleitung: Für ein Zwei-Phasen-Modell der Erzählanalyse. Ausdrucksform und Inhaltsform in mittelalterlichen und modernen Bearbeitungen der Gregoriuslegende', in: W. Haubrichs (ed.): *Erzählforschung 1. Theorien, Modelle und Methoden der Narrativik* [Zeitschrift für Literaturwissenschaft und Linguistik. Beiheft 4] (Göttingen 1976) 7-28.

Tomas Hägg, *Den antike romanen* (Uppsala 1980).

D. C. Hesseling, *Le roman de Phlorios et Platzia Phlore, publié avec une introduction, des observations et un index* par D. C. Hesseling [Verhandlingen der Koninklijke Akademie van Wetenschappen te Amsterdam, Afdeeling Letterkunde, N.R. 17.4] (Amsterdam 1917).

- , *L'Achilleide byzantine publiée avec une introduction, des observation et un index* [Verhandelingen der Koninklijke Akademie van Wetenschapen te Amsterdam, Afdeeling Letterkunde N.R.19.3] (Amsterdam 1919).

David Holton, Διήγησις τοῦ Ἀλεξάνδρου. *The Tale of Alexander. The Rhymed Version.* Critical edition with an introduction and commentary [Βυζαντινὴ καὶ νεοελληνικὴ βιβλιοθήκη 1] (Thessaloniki 1974).

- , '*Erotokritos* and Greek Tradition', in: R. Beaton (ed.), *The Greek Novel AD1-1985* (London 1988) 144-153.

H. Hunger, 'Zum Epilog der Theogonie des Johannes Tzetzes', BZ 46 (1953) 302-307.

- , 'Die byzantinische Literatur der Komnenenzeit. Versuch einer Neubewertung', Anzeiger der philos.-hist. Klasse der Österreichischen Akademie der Wissenschaften 105 (1968) 54-76 (reprint in *Byzantinische Grundlagenforschung* [London 1973]).

- , 'On the Imitation (Μίμησις) of Antiquity in Byzantine Literature', Dumbarton Oaks Papers 23-24 (1969-1970) 17-38.

- , *Die hochsprachliche profane Literatur der Byzantiner i-ii* [Handbuch der Altertumswissenschaft xii.1-2] (München 1978).

- , 'Stilstufen in der Geschichtsschreibung des 12. Jahrhunderts: Anna Komnena und Michael Glykas', Byzantine Studies 5 (1978) 139-170.

- , 'Die Herrschaft des Buchstabens. Das Verhältnis der Byzantiner zu Schrift- und Kanzleiwesen', Δελτίον τῆς Χριστιανικῆς 'Αρχαιολογικῆς 'Εταιρείας iv 12 (1984 [=1986]) 17-38 (reprint in *Epidosis. Gesammelte Schriften zur Byzantinischen Geistes- und Kulturgeschichte* [München 1989]).

- , *Schreiben und Lesen in Byzanz. Die byzantinische Buchkultur* [Beck's Archäologische Bibliothek] (München 1989).

W. Hörandner, *Theodoros Prodromos. Historische Gedichte* [Wiener Byzantinistische Studien 11] (Wien 1974).

David Jacoby, 'Quelques considerations sur la version de la "Chronique de Morée"', Journal des Savants 1968, 133-189.

H. R. Jauss, 'Literaturgeschichte als Provokation der Literaturwissenschaft', in: *Literaturgeschichte als Provokation* (Frankfurt a. M. 1970) 144-207.

- , *Ästhetische Erfahrung und literarisch Hermeneutik. I: Versuche im Feld der ästhetischen Erfahrung* (München 1977).

Elizabeth Jeffreys, 'Some Comments on the Manuscripts of *Imberios and Margarona*', Ἑλληνικά 27 (1974) 39-49.

- , 'The Manuscripts and Sources of the War of Troy'. *Actes du XIVe Congrès International des Études Byzantines (Bucarest, 6-12 Septembre 1971)*, publiés par les soins de M. Berza et E. Stanescu vol. III (Bucarest 1976) 91-94.

E. M. & M. J. Jeffreys, 'Imberios and Margarona: the manuscripts, sources and edition of a Byzantine verse romance', Byzantion 41 (1971) 122-160.

- , 'The Style of Byzantine Popular Poetry: Recent Work', in: *Okeanos. Essays presented to Ihor Ševčenko on his Sixtieth Birthday by his Colleagues and Students*. Edited by Cyril Mango and Omeljan Pritsak [Harvard Ukrainian Studies 7] (Cambridge, Mass. 1983) 309-343.

M. Jeffreys, 'The Chronicle of the Morea: Priority of the Greek Version', BZ 68 (1975) 304-350.

- , 'Digenis Akritas Manuscript Z', Δωδώνη 4 (1975) 163-201 (reprint in *Popular Literature in Late Byzantium* [London 1983])

Michael J. Jeffreys - Ole L. Smith, 'Political Verse for Queen Atossa', ClMed 42 (1991) 303-306.

Corinne Jouanno, *L'ekphrasis dans la littérature byzantine d'imagination* (Diss. Paris 1987).

E. D. **Kakoulidi**, 'Fior di virtù. "Ανθος Χαρίτων', Ελληνικά 24 (1971) 267-311.

A. **Karpozelos**, Συμβολή στη μελέτη του βίου και του έργου του Ιωάννη Μαυρόποδος [Δωδώνη, Παράρτημα 18] (Ioannina 1982).

A. P. **Kazhdan** - A. W. **Epstein**, Change in Byzantine Culture in the Eleventh and Twelfth Centuries (Berkeley - Los Angeles - London 1985).

A. P. **Kazhdan** - S. **Franklin**, Studies on Byzantine Literature of the Eleventh and Twelfth Centuries (Cambridge 1984).

A. P. **Kazhdan**, 'Certain Traits of Imperial Propaganda in the Byzantine Empire from the Eighth to the Fifteenth Centuries', in: Prédication et propagande au moyen âge. Islam, Byzance, Occident (Paris 1983).

- , 'The Aristocracy and the Imperial Ideal', in: M.Angold (ed.), The Byzantine Aristocracy ix to xiii Centuries [BAR International Series 221] (Oxford 1984).

G.**Kehagioglou**, Κριτική έκδοση της ιστορίας Πτωχολέοντος [Αριστοτέλειο Πανεπιστήμιο Θεσσαλονίκης. Επιστημονική επετηρίδα Φιλοσοφικής σχολής, Παράρτημα 22] (Thessaloniki 1978).

- , Review of **Beaton**, The Medieval Greek Romance, Ελληνικά 41 (1990) 158-171.

G. **Kennedy**, Greek Rhetoric under Christian Emperors (Princeton, N. J. 1983).

R. **Keydell**, 'Achilleis. Zur Problematik und Geschichte eines griechischen Romans', Byzantinische Forschungen 6 (1979) 83-99.

G. S. **Kirk**, The Songs of Homer (Cambridge 1962).

E. **Kirsten**, 'Die byzantinische Stadt', Berichte zum XI. Internationalen Byzantinistenkongress München 1958, V. 3. (München 1960).

E. **Kriaras**, Βυζαντινά ιπποτικά μυθιστορήματα [Βασική βιβλιοθήκη 2] (Athens 1955).

- , Λεξικό της μεσαιωνικής ελληνικής δημώδους γραμματείας 1100-1669. Τ. 1-11 (Thessaloniki 1969-1990).

- , 'Die zeitliche Einreihung des 'Phlorios und Platzia-Phlora'-Romans in Hinblick auf den 'Imberios und Margarona'-Roman'. Akten des XI. internationalen Byzantinistenkongresses München 1958 (München 1960) 269-272.

- , 'Η διγλωσσία στα υστεροβυζαντινά γράμματα και η διαμόρφωση των αρχών της νεοελληνικής λογοτεχνίας', Βυζαντινά 8 (1976) 215-243 (reprinted in: Μεσαιωνικά μελετήματα. Γραμματεία και γλώσσα, τόμος Β΄ [Thessaloniki 1988] 449-477).

St. **Kyriakidis**, 'Forschungsbericht zum Akritas-Epos', Berichte zum XI. Internationalen Byzantinistenkongress München 1958 II. 2. (München 1960).

J. A. **Lambert**, Le roman de Libistros et Rhodamné publié d'apres les manuscrits de Leyde et de Madrid avec une introduction, des observations grammaticales et un glossaire [Verhandelingen der koninklijke Akademie van Wetenschappen te Amsterdam. Afdeeling

Letterkunde, N.S.35.2] (Amsterdam1935).

Sp. Lambros, *Collection des Romans Grecs en langue vulgaire et en vers* (Paris 1880).

Renata Lavagnini, 'Note sull' Achilleide', Rivista di studi bizantini e neoellenici 6-7 (1969-70) 165-179.

- , *I Fatti di Troia. L'Iliade bizantina del cod. Paris. suppl. gr. 936.* Introduzione, traduzione e note di Renata Lavagnini [Quaderni dell' Istituto di filologia greca della universitá di Palermo 20] (Palermo 1988).

P. Lemerle, *Cinq études sur le xie siècle* (Paris 1977).

Alexandre Leupin, *Barbarolexis. Medieval Writing and Sexuality* (Cambridge, Mass. 1989).

St. Linnér, 'Psellus' Chronographia and the Alexias', BZ 76 (1983) 1-9.

A. R. Littlewood, 'Romantic paradises: the rôle of the garden in the Byzantine romance', BMGS 5 (1979) 95-114.

Paul Maas, 'Der byzantinische Zwölfsilber', BZ 12 (1903) 272-323.

- , 'Metrische Akklamationen der Byzantiner', BZ 21 (1912) 28-51.

- , *Textkritik,* in: A. Gercke - E. Norden, *Einleitung in die Altertumswissenschaft* Band I (Leipzig 1927). English translation by Barbara Flower (Oxford 1958).

E. V. Maltese, 'Anna Comnena nel mare delle sventure (Alex. xiv 7, 4)', BZ 80 (1987) 1-2.

Paul de Man, 'Genesis and Genealogy in Nietzsche's *Birth of Tragedy*', Diacritics 2.4 (1972) 44-53 (reprinted in *Allegories of Reading. Figural Language in Rousseau, Nietsche, Rilke and Proust* [New Haven 1979] 79-102).

- , 'Hypogram and Inscription: Michael Riffaterre's Poetics of Reading', Diacritics 11.4 (1981) 17-35 (reprinted in *The Resistance to Theory*, forword by Wlad Godzich [Theory and History of Literature 33] [Minneapolis 1986] 27-53).

Cyril Mango, *Byzantine Literature as a Distorting Mirror* (Oxford 1975).

- , *Byzantium. The empire of New Rome* (London 1980).

A. Markopoulos, 'Η οργάνωση του σχολείου. Παράδοση και εξέλιξη', in: *Η καθημερινή ζωή στο Βυζάντιο. Τομές και συνέχειες στην ελληνιστική και ρωμαϊκή παράδοση*. Πρακτικά του Α΄ διεθνούς συμποσίου 15-17 Σεπτεμβρίου 1988 (Athens 1989) 325-333.

- , 'Ο Διγενής Ακρίτης και η βυζαντινή χρονογραφία. Μία πρώτη προσέγγιση', Αριάδνη 5 (1989) 165-171.

Karl Meister, *Die homerische Kunstsprache* (Leipzig 1921).

Reinhold Merkelbach, *Roman und Mysterium in der Antike* (München & Berlin 1962).

D. Michailidis, '*Palamedes rediens*. La fortuna di Palamede nel medioevo ellenico', Rivista di studi bizantini e neoellenici 8-9 (1971-1972) 261-280.

K. Mitsakis, Προβλήματα σχετικά μὲ τὸ κείμενο, τὶς πηγὲς καὶ τὴ χρονολόγηση τῆς

Αχιλληίδος (Thessaloniki 1961) (reprinted in *Το εμψυχούν ύδωρ. Μελέτες μεσαιωνικής και νεοελληνικής φιλολογίας* [Κριτική-Μελετήματα 7] [Athens 1983] 389-464).

Gareth Morgan, 'Cretan Poetry: Sources and Inspiration', Κρητικά χρονικά 14 (1960) 44-68.

Lars Nørgaard, 'Byzantine Romance - Some Remarks on the Coherence of Motives', ClMed 40 (1989) 271-294.

Lars Nørgaard - Ole L. Smith, *A Byzantine Iliad. The Text of* Par. Suppl. Gr. *926. Edited with critical apparatus, introduction and indices* [Opuscula graeco-latina edenda curavit Ivan Boserup vol. 5] (Copenhagen 1975).

Paolo Odorico, 'La sapienza del Digenis. Materiali per lo studio dei *loci similes* nella recensione di Grottaferrata', Byzantion 59 (1989) 137-163.

N. Oikonomides, 'L' "épopée" de Digénis et la frontière orientale de Byzance aux Xe et XIe siècles', Travaux & Mémoires 7 (1979) 375-397.

Birgit Olsen, 'The Greek Translation of Boccaccio's *Theseid* Book 6', ClMed 41 (1990) 273-301.

Annaclara Cataldi Palau, 'La tradition manuscrite d' Eustathe Makrembolitès', Revue d'Histoire de Textes 10 (1980) 75-113.

N. M. Panagiotakis, *Τὸ κείμενο τῆς πρώτης ἐκδόσης τοῦ " Ἀπόκοπου". Τυπογραφικὴ καὶ φιλολογικὴ διερεύνηση* (Venice 1991).

Th. Ph. Papadopoulos, 'Κορακιστικά', Μεγάλη ἑλληνικὴ ἐγκυκλοπαίδεια 14 (1931) 867-868.

M. Papathomopoulos, 'L'édition critique du Πόλεμος της Τρωάδος. Problèmes méthodologiques', in: H. Eideneier (ed.), *Neograeca Medii Aevi*, 279-283.

G. Pasquali, *Storia della tradizione e critica del testo* (2. ed. Firenze 1962).

Michel Pichard, *Le Roman de Callimaque et de Chrysorrhoé*. Texte établi et traduit (Paris 1956).

A. Pignani, *Nicephoro Basilace. Progimnasmi e monodie* [Byzantina e Neo-Hellenica Neapolitana. Collana di studi e testi 10] (Napoli 1983).

Maria Politi-Sakellariadi, 'Προβλήματα τῆς ἐκδόσης του " Λόγου Παρηγορητικού περὶ Δυστυχίας καὶ Εὐτυχίας", in: H. Eideneier (ed.), *Neograeca medii aevi* , 285-293.

L. Politis, 'Νεοελληνική (βυζαντινὴ καί νεωτέρα) μετρική', Μεγάλη ἑλληνικὴ ἐγκυκλοπαίδεια 17 (1931) 101-103.

- , 'L'épopée byzantine de Digenis Akritas', *Atti del convegno internazionale sul tema: La poesia epica e la sua formazione*. Accademia Nazionale dei Lincei 357, 1970, Quaderno no. 139, 551-581.

- , 'Venezia come centro della stampa e della diffusione della prima letteratura neoellenica', in: *Venezia centro di mediazione tra oriente e occidente (secoli xv-xvi). Aspetti e problemi* (Firenze 1977) 443-479.

I. K. Promponas, Ἀκριτικά Α΄ (Athens 1985).

Stefan Radt, *Tragicorum graecorum fragmenta* 4: Sophocles (Göttingen 1977).

D. R. Reinsch, review of **A. Pignani**, BZ 80 (1987) 89-91.

- , 'Ausländer und Byzantiner im Werk der Anna Komnene', Rechtshistorisches Journal 8 (1989) 257-274.

M. Riffaterre, *La production du texte* (Paris 1979).

- , *Fictional Truth* (Baltimore 1990).

H. Saradi-Mendelovici, 'The Demise of the Ancient City and the Emergence of the Medieval City in the Eastern Roman Empire', Classical Views n. s. 7 (1988) 365-401.

Bjarne Schartau, *Codices graeci Haunienses. Ein deskriptiver Katalog des griechischen Handschriftenbestandes der Königlichen Bibliothek Kopenhagen* (forthcoming).

H. Schreiner, 'Zerrissene Zusammenhänge und Fremdkörper im Belthandros-Text', BZ 52 (1959) 257-264.

- , 'Der älteste Imberiostext', *Akten des XI. internationalen Byzantinistenkongresses München 1958* (München 1960) 556-562.

- , 'Die zeitliche Aufeinanderfolge der im cod. Vind. Theol. gr. 244 überlieferten Texte des Imberios, des Belisar und des Florios, und ihr Schreiber', BZ 55 (1962) 213-223.

- , 'Die einleitenden Überschriften zu den von der gleichen Hand übelieferten Texten in Cod. Neap. Gr. III. AA. 9 und Cod. Neap. Gr. III. B. 27', Byzantinische Forschungen 1 (1966) 290-320.

Ihor Ševčenko, ' Levels of Style in Byzantine Prose', JÖB 31.1 (1981) 290-312.

- , 'Additional Remarks to the Report', JÖB 32.1 (1982) 220-229.

A. Sigalas, *Mélanges Merlier* ii (Athénes 1956) 355-377.

Ole L. Smith, 'Tricliniana', ClMed 33 (1981-1982) 239-262.

- , 'Anonymus Mutinensis or Andronikos Kallistos?', ClMed 37 (1986) 255-258.

- , 'Notes on the Byzantine Achilleid. The Oxford Version', ClMed 39 (1988) 259-272.

- , *The Byzantine Achilleid: The Oxford Version* [Opuscula graecolatina edenda curavit Ivan Boserup vol. 32] (Copenhagen 1990).

K. Snipes, 'The *Chronographia* of Michael Psellos and the Textual Tradition and Transmission of the Byzantine Historians of the Eleventh and Twelfth Centuries', Zbornik Radova 27/28 (1989) 43-62.

G. Spadaro, 'Note critiche ed esegetiche al testo greco di "Florio e Plaziaflora"', Byzantion 33 (1963) 449-472.

- , *Contributi sulle fonte del romanzo greco-medievale "Florio e Plaziaflora"* [Κείμενα καὶ μελέται νεοελληνικῆς φιλολογίας 26] (Athens 1966).

- , 'Per una nuova edizione di Florios ke Platziaflore', BZ 67 (1974) 64-73.

- , 'Sul Teseida Neogreco', Folia Neohellenica 2 (1977) 157-160.

- , 'Testi medievali greci in demotico tramandati in codici napolitani', Ιταλοελληνικά 1 (1988) 49-74.

Alfredo Stussi (ed.), *La critica del testo* (Bologna 1985).

B. Tatakis, *Βυζαντινή φιλοσοφία* (Athens[4] 1977).

J. Tatum - Gail M. Vernazza (ed.), *The Ancient Novel. Classical Paradigms and Modern Perspectives*. Proceedings of the 2nd International Conference on the Ancient Novel [Dartmouth College, 23-29 July 1989] (Hanover, N. H. 1990).

Marcelle Thiébaux, *The Stag of Love. The Chase in Medieval Literature* (Ithaca, N. Y. 1974).

Erich Trapp, *Digenes Akrites. Synoptische Ausgabe der ältesten Versionen* [Wiener Byzantinistische Studien 8] (Wien 1971).

Isavella Tsavari, *Ὁ Πουλολόγος. Κριτικὴ ἔκδοση μὲ εἰσαγωγή, σχόλια καὶ λεξιλόγιο* [Βυζαντινὴ καὶ νεοελληνικὴ βιβλιοθήκη 5] (Athens 1987).

Aleksander Turyn, *Dated Greek Manuscripts in the Libraries of Italy* 1 (Urbana - Chicago - London 1972).

A. van Gemert, *Μαρίνου Φαλιέρου Ἐρωτικὰ ὄνειρα. Κριτικὴ ἔκδοση μὲ εἰσαγωγή, σχόλια καὶ λεξιλόγιο* [Βυζαντινὴ καὶ νεοελληνικὴ βιβλιοθήκη 4] (Thessaloniki 1980).

- , 'Η Αχιλληίδα και η ιστορία του Βελισαρίου', Ελληνικά 33 (1981) 82-97.

Ebbe Vilborg, *Achilles Tatius, Leucippe and Clitophon. A Commentary* [Studia Graeca et latina Gothoburgensia xv] (Acta Universitatis Gothoburgensis, Stockholm 1962).

G. Wagner, *Carmina graeca medii aevi* (Lipsiae 1874).

H. M. Wehrhahn, *Übersichtstabellen zur handschriftlichen Überlieferung der Gedichte Gregors von Nazianz* (Aachen 1967).

René Wellek, 'The Concept of Realism in Literary Scholarship', Neophilologus 44 (1960) 1-20 (reprint in: *Concepts of Criticism* [Yale 1963] 222-255).

D. J. Wilcox, *The Measure of Times Past. Pre-Newtonian Chronologies and the Rhetoric of Relative Time* (Chicago 1987).

Th. N. Zeses, *Γεννάδιος Β´ Σχολάριος. Βίος, συγγράμματα, διδασκαλία* [Ἀνάλεκτα Βλατάδων 30] (Thessaloniki 1980).

INDEX LOCORUM

Achilleid L: **527**: 24
Achilleid N: **9-19**: 102f; **20-28**: 97; **20**: 98; **283-298**: 62; **790**: 24; **794**: 24; **813**: 46; **816-20**: 46; **818**: 47; **843-78**: 85; **1045-47**: 62; **1195**: 62; **1798-1811**: 106; **1804**: 106
Achilleid O : **184**: 103; **268**: 103; **422**: 103; **566**: 103; **661**: 103
Achilleus Tatios i 17-18: 77
Apollonios Rhodios: *Arg.* i 721-768: 42
Aristophanes : *Aves* 695: 81

Byzantine Iliad: **9**: 98; **56-64**: 24; **64**: 24; **202** rubr.: 69; **259** rubr.: 69; **391-92**: 63; **442ff**: 63; **493-96**: 105; **503**ff: 63; **520-21**: 63; **530**: 63; **590ff**: 63; **615f**: 63; **661f**: 63; **795-99**: 105; **886-88**: 105; **887**: 103; **1060-71**: 105; **1110-11**: 103
Belthandros **1-3**: 103; **235**: 62; **281**:86; **327**: 86; **432**: 86; **441**: 86.

Cantare di Fiorio e Biancifiore st. 91: 96

Digenis E **791-92**: 31; **835**: 31
Digenis G **iv 241-53**: 31; **970**: 30; **967**: 30; **vi 837**: 30
Digenis Z **1-7**: 109

Eustathios Makrembolites, *Hysmine and Hysminias* **ix 23, 3**: 39; **ix 22**: 43; **ii 7, 2-3**: 82

Florios and Platziaflora **63** rubr.: 68; **110** rubr.: 68; **111**: 103; **190-194**: 46; **191**: 47; **276**: 103; **646**: 103; **788** rubr.: 69; **832** rubr.: 68; **1048** rubr.: 68; **1193-95**: 96f; **1391**: 103; **1591**: 103

Georgios Scholarios iii 253, 1-6: 16f
Gregorios Nazianzenos *de vita sua* : 79

Hesych. A7539: 82

Imberios and Margarona **230-33**: 97; **483**: 100
Ioannes Mauropous 165-178: 17

Kallimachos and Chrysorrhoe **449-455**: 78f; **781-82**: 81; **852-59**: 104; **2457-68**: 81; **2606-09**: 107
Konstantinos Manasses: fr. 21-21a: 77

Leo Grammatikos 252, 5-8: 16
Livistros and Rhodamne E **849-857**: 84; **1192**: 87; **1191-92**: 87f
Livistros and Rhodamne N **161-171**: 77; **269**: 86; **293-304**: 84; **298-99**: 84; **513-519**: 84; **528**: 82; **531**: 82; **693-698**:84; **711-14**: 84; **711-29**: 84; **725-29**: 84; **1040-41**: 88
Livistros and Rhodamne P**577-84**: 84; **1125-1393**: 88
Livistros and Rhodamne S **61-68**: 87; **63-64**: 88f; **63**: 89;**65**: 88 **196-211**: 84; **278-79**: 89; **439**: 89; **634-35**: 54; **1433-1513**: 88; **1922-1920**: 79; **1925**: 79;**1926**: 79; **2432-2463**: 78; **2891-2898**: 54
Livistros and Rhodamne V f. 42-43r: 88f

Maiuri poem 64-66: 47

Nikephoros Basilakes, *Progymn.* vii 26: 23; vii 27: 23
Nikephoros Bryennios i 16: 37; 17: 15; ii 24: 40
Niketas Eugenianos,*Drosilla and Charikles* **ii 216-19**: 81; **248**: 11; **382**: 81; **iii 17**: 42; **iv 135-49**: 77; **iv 412**: 80

Photios *Bibl.* ii 11 : 39; ii 34: 39
Psellos, *Chron.* viib 22-23: 15

Sappho fr. 44 L.-P.: 41
Schol. Aesch. *Pers.* 155-158: 49
Sophokles fr. 871 Radt: 39

Theodoros Meliteniotes 176, 10-11: 15
Theodoros Metochites. *misc.* 625-642: 18
Theodoros Prodromos 38 (Hör.): 19
- , *Rhodanthe and Drosikles*: **ii 249-50**: 42; **iv 329-411**: 42; **ix 320ff**: 42; **ix 336**: 42
Theseid proem. : 97

SUBJECT INDEX

acheiropoietos: 24
Achilleid: 27, 28, 31, 46, 48, 52, 54-5, 56, 58, 59, 60, 62-3, 67, 77, 80, 83, 85, 91-2, 94, 95, 96, 97-8, 100, 101, 102-4, 106, 108, 109, 110
Achilles: 62-3, 67, 69, 85, 105
Achilleus Tatios: 20, 41, 77, 80
Adler, Max: 39
Aeschylus: 49, 52
aesthetics: 74
Agapitos, P. A.: 13, 24, 28, 37, 38, 39, 40, 52, 56, 58, 59, 69, 75, 77, 78, 79, 81, 82, 84, 86, 88, 96
akropolis: 86
Akritis: 72
Aleksidze, A. D.: 10
Alexander-story: 26, 71, 72
Alexios I Komnenos: 39, 40
Alexiou, Margaret: 20, 38, 49
Alexiou, Stylianos: 28, 29, 31, 52
allegory: 107
allusions: 36, 41
de Andrés, G.: 28, 29, 30
Andromeda: 80
Andronikos Kallistos: 93
Andronikos Noukios: 110
Andronikos Palaiologos: 48, 55
Angold, Michael: 32
'Angst' Byzantine: 34
'Angst', male: 81
Anna Komnene: 19, 27, 39, 67
Anonymus Mutinensis: 93
antiquarianism, Byzantine: 33, 36
apatheia: 39
Aphthonios: 22
Aphrodite: 41, 76
apocrypha: 27
Apokopos: 52, 72
Apostolopoulos, Ph.: 20
Arab(s): 20, 26, 75
archetype: 69, 92, 100
Arcita: 72
Arethas: 35
Argyrokastron: 62, 86, 87, 89
Aristophanes: 46, 93
Aristotle: 35, 40
Armenian: 16
art: 41-2
Artykomis: 82
audience, fictional: 62

Auerbach, Erich: 10
'authentication': 18
author/copyist: 91, 99, 109
author (persona): 42-4
authorial interjections: 78
awareness, Byzantine: 12

Bakker, Wim F.: 52, 91, 92-5, 108
Barthes, Roland: 73
Bartsch, Shadi: 42, 77
Basileios I: 16
Basileios of Kaisareia: 19
basileus: 37
basilikos logos: 27
bath: 76, 81
Beck, Hans-Georg: 9, 10, 22, 27, 30, 39, 46, 48, 55, 57, 61, 68, 71, 82, 85, 94, 108
bedchambers: 62, 80, 87-9
di Benedetto, Anna Zimbone: 66
Belisarios: 27, 52, 91-102, 95, 104, 108, 109
Belthandros and Chrysantza: 24, 52, 57-8, 61, 69, 77, 81, 83, 86, 88, 98, 103, 104
Benoît de St. Maure: 85, 100
binding: 30
biography: 27, 33
Boccaccio: 65, 92
borrowings, literary: 91
Boulenger, F.: 19
Bowie, E .L.: 34
'breaks', historical: 12-3, 15, 26
Browning, Robert: 17, 47
Bryer, A.: 15
Busbeck, Augerius: 68
Byzantine Iliad: 52, 55, 60-1, 63-4, 69, 77, 83, 98, 103, 104, 104-5, 109
Byzantinisches Handbuch: 13, 22
Byzantinists: 9

canonization: 44
Cantare di Fiorio e Biancifiore: 96
Cantarella, Eva: 81
castles: 63, 85-90
Cataldi Palau, Annaclara: 66
causality: 39
Cerquiglini, B.: 9
Chance; see *Tyche*
chapbook: 65, 70, 72, 92, 100
chariot: 84
Chariton: 61, 80
Charon: 38, 76
chateau d' amour: 85, 87
Chatman, S.: 50
Chatzigiakoumis, Manolis K.: 10, 30, 55, 56, 57, 58, 100, 104
cherubim: 84
Cheynet, J. C.: 15
Christ: 37

Christian(s): 19
Chronicle of the Morea: 27, 44-6
chronology: 9, 28, 45, 50, 60, 67, 71, 84, 105
Cirignano, John: 93
citizenship, Byzantine: 16
Claude, D.: 86
codicology: 10
comparative studies: 10, 58
compound words: 46
Constantinople: 13, 15, 28, 32, 46, 51, 66, 68, 79, 81, 108, 109
contamination: 101
copyists; see scribes
coupe de foudre: 76
court, imperial: 48, 56, 67, 83, 106
Courtonne, Yves: 19
Crete: 13, 29, 70, 110-1
criticism, literary 13, 34, 58, 73-75, 79
Cupane, Carolina: 77, 82, 83-7, 90
Curtius, Ernst Robert: 10
Dain, Alphonse: 92
Danezis, Georg: 48
dating; see chronology
death scenes: 38, 79
Dedes, D.: 24
Demetrios (scribe): 93
Derrida, Jacques: 74
description; see *ekphrasis*
determination, divine: 39
Deuling, Judy K.: 93
dialects: 29
Dieu d'amour: 83
Digenis : 28-33, 40, 45, 49, 56, 76, 80, 85, 92, 108, 109
diglossia: 19
Dimitrios Zinos: 70-2, 92-3
Dionysos: 41
Dodds, Eric R.: 34
dominance, cultural: 13
Drakontokastron: 86
drama: 39-40
dreams: 84

East/West interaction: 20, 24, 49, 75-6, 81-90, 108
editions, modern: 10, 97, 99
editorial practice, modern: 9-10, 58, 87-9, 97-98
education, Byzantine: 22, 35, 36, 42, 75, 77, 80
Eideneier, Hans: 10, 48
ekphrasis: 24, 32, 41, 46, 76, 77
ekplexis: 78
eleos: 40
Eliot, T. S.: 73
elopement-motif: 40
emperor; see imperial imagery
'entertainment' literature: 19, 22

Ephraim the Syrian: 16
Epstein, Anne W.: 15, 16
Eros: 37, 38, 62, 75, 76, 77, 81, 82, 83-5, 86, 87
Erotokastron: 86
Erotokritos: 111
erudition: 75, 77
ethos: 39
Eustathios (*Digenis Z*): 109-10
Eustathios Makrembolites: 23, 39, 42-4, 66, 75, 76, 77, 82, 85, 84, 87, 110
Eustathios of Thessalonike: 49
exemplar; see *Vorlage*

fables: 26
falcon-hunting: 82
Falieros, Marinos: 48, 54, 109-10
Fate; see *Tyche*
Ferry, L.: 76
Fleischmann, Suzanne: 9
Florios and Platziaflora: 46, 48, 51, 58, 65, 67-70, 91, 95, 96-7, 100, 103
Foley, John M.: 98
Follieri, Enrica: 65, 70, 71, 93
folklore: 83
folk songs: 57, 76
Foss, Clive: 86
Foucault, Michel: 74
Franklin, Simon: 15, 25
Fuhrmann, M.: 93
Fyrigos, A.: 48

Gallay, P.: 66
Gamillscheg, Ernst: 30, 71, 93, 110
garden: 23, 87
Garland, Lynda: 57, 61
Gaselee, S.: 20
Gautier, P.: 67
van Gemert, A.: 52, 54, 91, 92-95, 108, 110
'genealogy': 73-5, 77, 79, 89
Genette, Gerard: 14, 50
genre: 50-1
Georgios Scholarios: 16
Giatromanolakis, G.: 39
Gier, A.: 9
Greece, feudal: 13
Greek Anthology: 38
Greek themes: 65, 70
Gregorios Nazianzenos: 38, 66, 79-80
Grumel, Venance: 13
Grunebaum, G. E. von: 19

Haag, Benedikt: 55, 67
Hägg, Tomas: 20
hagiography: 26-7, 80
Hamon, Philippe: 77

happy end: 40
Harlfinger, Dieter: 71, 93, 110
Haubrichs, Walter: 50
hearers: 102
Helen: 63
Hellenes (pagans): 16
Hellenocentricity: 16
Heliodoros: 36, 41, 76, 80
hermeneutics: 10
Hermes: 43
Hermogenes: 22
Heron of Alexandria: 67
Hesiod: 110
Hesseling, D. C. : 54, 68, 69, 98, 103
Hesychios: 82
hexameter: 31
historiography: 26-7
Hörandner, Wolfram: 19, 26
Holton, David: 49, 70, 71, 111
Homer: 36, 60, 105, 107
Hunger, Herbert: 10, 16, 19, 20, 22, 23, 30, 38, 44, 76, 94
hypothesis: 39
Hysmine: 82
Hysminias: 43

iambic trimeter: 37, 49
iconography: 84
icons: 24
'identity, national': 15, 19, 26
Iliad: 98
Imberios and Margarona: 51, 69, 70, 71, 91, 95, 96-7, 100, 108, 111
imperial imagery: 37, 77, 81, 85, 86
'inactivity'; see *apatheia*
initiation pattern: 38
'innovation': 25
interpolations: 54, 96
intertextuality: 36, 73-4, 89
Ioannes Chrysostomos: 38, 47
Ioannes Gregoropoulos: 93
Ioannes Italos: 35
Ioannes Skylitzes: 87
Ioannes Tzetzes: 16
Iser, Wolgang: 14

Jacoby, David: 45, 46
Jauss, Hans Robert: 14, 73, 77, 106
Jeffreys, Elizabeth M.: 29, 52, 65, 70, 71, 91, 95, 96, 98, 100
Jeffreys, Michael J.: 29, 45, 49, 52, 70, 91, 95, 96, 98, 100, 108
Jews: 16
Jungck, Ch.: 79
Jouanno, Corinne: 77

Kahane, Renée & Henry: 72, 77

Kallimachos and Chrysorrhoe: 19, 24, 46, 48, 55-6, 58, 61, 75, 76, 80, 81, 83, 85, 86, 98, 104, 106-8
katouna: 86
Kazhdan, Alexander P.: 15, 16, 25
Kechagioglou, G,: 54, 112
Kennedy, George: 23
Kirk, G. S.: 99
Kirsten, E.: 86
Klitovon: 62, 84
Kriaras, E.: 19, 24, 57, 67, 68, 69, 96, 97
Krumbacher, Karl: 67
Komnenian works: 13, 37, 42-4, 77-80
Komnenoi: 15, 34, 39, 40
Konstantinos Manasses: 39, 55, 77
Konstantinos IX Monomachos: 85
Kornaros, Ventzentios: 111
Kunstsprache: 46-7, 98-9
Kyriakidis, Stilpon: 29

Lachmann, Karl: 100
language, spoken: 15, 16, 19, 46, 57
language, vernacular: 18, 27, 28, 31, 32, 45, 46-48, 57, 83, 88-89, 99
Lambert, Jacoba A.: 59, 79, 88
Lambropoulos, V.: 74
Lambros, Sp. P.: 55
Late Antiquity: 20
Latin(s): 16, 20, 82-3
Lavagnini, Renata: 24, 54, 55, 60
Lemerle, Paul: 15
Lendari, Tina: 59
Leon Choirosphaktes: 35
letters: 87
Leupin, Alexander: 41
Lilla, Salvatore: 94
linguistics: 10, 12, 47, 58, 76, 99
Linnér, St.: 67
literature, Modern Greek: 13
literature, Oriental; see Arab(s)
Littlewood, A. R.: 23, 87
Livistros and Rhodamne: 24, 28, 30, 52, 56, 58-9, 62, 69, 77, 80, 83, 86, 87-9, 92, 94, 104, 108
lizios: 83
loan-words, Italian: 60
Lord, Albert B.: 46, 100

Maas, Paul: 31, 101
Maiuri, A.: 19, 47
Maltese, E. V.: 67
de Man, Paul: 41, 74-5
Mango, Cyril: 11, 15, 22, 27
Manuel Moschopoulos: 110
Manuel Philes: 55-6, 106-8
manuscript collectors: 20, 66, 94, 99

manuscripts (general): 10, 20, 21, 29, 51, 58, 65, 66-7, 100, 104, 108, 110
manuscripts (individual):
    Bologna 3567: 98
    Copenhagen, *Fabr.* 57: 45
    Escorial T.ii.18: 71
    Escorial Ψ. iv.22: 28, 329, 59, 88, 94, 95
    Florence, Bibl. Laur. 86, 3: 49
    Grottaferrata Z.a.44: 28
    Leiden, *Scalig.* 55: 56-7, 59, 88
    Leningrad 741: 93
    London, B.M. *Add.* 8241: 27, 54, 59, 67, 68, 98
    Modena, Bibl. Est. gr. 241: 52
    Naples, Bibl. Naz. iii.Aa.9: 54, 59
    Naples, Bibl. Naz. iii.B.27: 27, 55, 59, 70, 91-92, 94, 97, 108, 110
    Oxford, Bodl. Libr. *Auct.* T.5.24: 55, 59
    Oxford, Bodl. Libr. *misc.* 287: 70, 97
    Paris, Bibl. Nat. *Coisl.* 344: 98
    Paris, Bibl. Nat. *gr.* 1712: 66
    Paris, Bibl. Nat. *gr.* 2038: 94
    Paris, Bibl. Nat. *gr.* 2898: 27, 46, 71, 92, 100
    Paris, Bibl. Nat. *gr.* 2909: 57, 96
    Paris, Bibl. Nat. *Suppl.gr.* 926: 60
    Selest. 347: 94
    Vat. gr..1139: 52
    Vat. gr. .2214: 94
    Vat. gr. 2391: 59, 88
    Vat. Palat. gr. 426: 70-2, 92, 97, 100
    Vienna, *theol. gr.:* 244: 31, 67, 68, 70, 72, 93, 97
manuscript trade; see manuscript collectors
manuscript tradition: 27, 29, 50-61, 100-1
Markopoulos, A.: 33, 36
Martiniani-Reber, Marielle: 82
Maximos Planoudes: 49
Maximou: 30
Meister, Karl: 46
Menander Rhetor; 27
Menelaos: 63
Merkelbach, Reinhold: 35
metre: 32, 49
Michael III: 16
Michael VIII: 58
Michael Attaleiates: 15
Michael Psellos: 15, 27, 35, 38, 66, 78, 85
Michailidis, D.: 54, 91
Medievalists: 9
mimesis: 37, 42-4, 62, 73
monkey: 76
Morgan, Gareth: 29, 111
Musurus, Markos: 93
Myrtane: 62
mythology: 41, 80, 107

names: 80

Narcissus: 77
narration, first-person: 23, 31, 77, 108
narrative content: 50
narrative discourse: 50
narrative transitions: 31
narrator (persona): 42-3
nationality: 16
nature: 41-2
Nicolini da Sabio: 65
night: 76
Nikephoros Basilakes: 23, 87
Nikephoros Bryennios: 17, 27, 40, 67
Niketas David Paphlagon: 35
Niketas Eugenianos: 37, 39, 76, 81, 83
Nikolaos (rhetorician): 23
Nikolaos Kalliergis: 72
Nikolaos Sophianos: 94
Nørgaard, Lars: 55, 57
novels, ancient: 23, 34, 38, 107

Odorico, Paolo: 30
Odyssey: 30, 98
Oikonomidès. N.: 32
Olsen, Birgit: 65, 70, 71, 93
orality: 32, 33, 57, 92, 95, 100

pagan(s): 20, 35, 40, 117
Panagiotakis, N. M.: 78
Pandrouklos: 67
Papadopoulos, Th. Ph.: 50
Papathomopoulos, M.: 71
paradoxon: 45
parainesis: 46
Paris (hero): 65, 68
Parry, Milman: 48, 108
Pasquali, G.: 110
pathos: 41
patterns, structural: 12
Peri Distichias ke Eftichias: 118
Persian: 16
philosophy: 35-7
Philostratos: 44
phobos: 42
Photios: 36, 41
phylladion; see chapbook
Pichard, Michel: 59, 60, 63, 83, 110
Pignani, Adriana: 23
Pindar 121
plagiarism: 106
Plato: 36, 100
Plutarch: 27, 41, 43
polis: 94
political verse: 32

Politi-Sakellariadi, Maria: 118
Politis, L.: 28, 30, 32, 51, 77
Pontic: 29
pools: 66
popular: 27, 50, 62
popularity: 20, 27, 71
Poulologos: 10, 47
printing: 70, 77
process, historical: 12
progymnasmata: 23, 44, 84
Promponas, I. K.: 29, 82
proverbs: 49-50
Ptochoprodromika: 10, 19, 20, 49
public; see readers
Pythian oracle: 80

readers, Byzantine: 20-1, 72, 111-6, 117
reading, silent: 21
realism: 25
reception: 71, 81, 116-22
register, linguistic; see style
Reinsch, Dieter R.: 23
'renaissance': 16, 46
Renault, A.: 81
Rezeptionsästhetik: 80, 84, 116
Rezeptionsgeschichte: 116
rhetoric: 22-5, 28, 41-2, 44-6, 84-6, 111-3
Rhetorica ad Alexandrum: 102
Riffaterre, Michael: 43
river: 88
romances, study of: 13
Roman de la Rose: 23
Roman de Troie: 70
Romanos the Melodist: 24
rubrics: 61, 74-5

'salvation'-motif: 35, 37, 39, 40, 45-6
Sappho: 43
Satradi-Mendelovici, H.: 93
Sardis: 93
Sathas, K. N.: 73, 102
Schartau, Bjarne: 48
Schirò, G.: 102
Schmidt, W.: 72
scholar/scribe: 101-2, 121
Schreiner, Hugo: 31, 59, 61, 75, 77, 102, 105, 110
scribes: 29, 31, 54, 60, 64, 73, 74, 99, 100-10, 117, 120
Scythian: 16
Second Sophistic: 23
'self-consciousness, Byzantine': 26, 33, 34, 42, 50
semioticians: 43
seraphim: 91
set-piece, dramatic: 41-2

Ševčenko, Ihor: 19
sexuality: 32, 66, 7-8, 91, 94, 96
Sicherl, Martin: 102
Sigalas, A.: 61
Smith, Ole L.: 32, 52, 59, 65, 66, 68, 102, 112
Snipes. K.: 37
Sophocles: 41, 102
Spadaro, Giuseppe: 50, 58, 72, 73, 74, 75, 99, 105-7
Spaneas: 50, 55
speech frame: 62
stemma: 55, 63, 71, 75, 100, 104, 110
storm scenes: 86
Stussi, Alfredo: 10
style, levels of: 19, 49, 116
stylistics: 25, 33, 82
subtitles; see rubrics
symbolism: 95
Syntipas: 27
Syriac: 16

Tarsos: 66
Tatum, J.: 66
textual history: 10, 121
thematic similarity: 86-7
Thanatos: 40
Theodoros Meliteniotes: 92, 118
Theodoros Prodromos: 19, 27, 33, 38, 44-5, 48, 49, 83, 85
Theodoros Stypiotes: 19
theology: 36, 92
theory, literary; see criticism
Theseid: 27, 48, 54, 70, 76-8, 101, 1o6-7, 110, 121
Thiébaux, Marcelle: 97
Thousand and One Nighs: 88
throne: 91
Thurn, H.: 72
Timarion: 37
time, concept of: 12-3
tragedy: 42
translations: 70-8
transliteration: 11
transposition, linguistic: 50, 62
Trapp, Erich: 28, 31, 119
tricolon abundans: 85
Trivialliteratur: 22
trochaic tetrameter: 52
Tsavari, Isavella: 10, 102
Turyn, Aleksander: 121
Tuscan *Florios*: 73, 75
Tyche: 36, 40, 86

Venice: 13, 70, 76, 101
vernacular; see language
Vernazza, Gail M.: 66

Vilborg, Ebbe: 21
virgins, dangling: 88
virginity: 68
Volk, Robert: 36
Vorlage: 64, 73, 77, 100-1, 103

Wagner, Wilhelm: 102
Waltharius: 13
Walz, C.: 23
War of Troy: 54, 71, 106-7, 110
watermarks: 30, 47, 58, 60, 77, 121
Wehrhahn, H. M.: 72
Wellek, Rene: 25
Wessel, Klaus: 90
Wilcox, D. J.: 13
Wilson, Nigel G.: 20
Winfield, D.: 93
wonder-tale: 90, 91
wordplay: 85
world, fictional: 90-1

Xanthoudidis, St.: 29, 59
Xenophon Ephesios: 42-3

Zacharias Kalliergis: 102